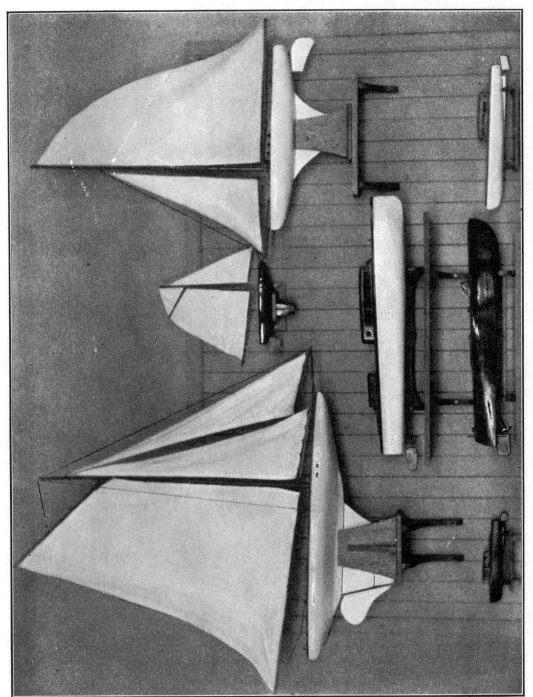

Model Sailing Yachts and Model Motor Boats made in the Bryant Junior High School, Minneapolis

BOATS, AIRPLANES, and KITES

BY

ARMAND J. LABERGE

Instructor of Manual Arts
BRYANT JUNIOR HIGH SCHOOL
MINNEAPOLIS, MINNESOTA

Assistant Supervisor of Playgrounds, During the
Summer Months, Minneapolis Park Board

THE MANUAL ARTS PRESS
PEORIA, ILLINOIS

Boats, Airplanes and Kites

by Armand J LaBerge

Originally published by
Manual Arts Press
Peoria

Original Copyright 1935
by Armand J LaBerge

Reprinted by
Lindsay Publications Inc
Bradley IL 60915

ISBN 1-55918-302-X

2003

1   2   3   4   5   6   7   8   9   0

WARNING

INTRODUCTION

IN THE press of business or industrial life it is not surprising that inadequate account has sometimes been taken of the emotional factors, as well as the numerous characteristics and impulses which enter into human behavior and performance. The wise man of practical affairs, however, has come to learn that wherever a contact is made with the consumer, it pays to make things attractive as well as useful, to be pleasant rather than austere, and in general to build upon the interests of the prospect, even if those interests have to be stimulated or created in some instances.

Commercial interests have come to such a recognition as a matter of making a better market for the products of industry, commerce, and business. Persons who pride themselves on being educators are aiming, presumably, toward the general improvement and betterment of the human race, and of conditions which affect them. In working toward this end, school people have not always lived up to the best standard in the matter of building upon valuable human interests.

The field of industrial education, particularly in the elementary and junior high school, permits of procedure in two diametrically opposite directions. On the one hand, if the *person* in charge lacks imagination, and appreciation of human impulses, the manipulative work may consist in unrelated exercises or stilted projects, completed largely for the sake of the technical accomplishment involved. On the other hand, the *teacher* who possesses a knowledge of child interests, a vivid memory of his own childhood impulses and interests, and a keen appreciation of the value of individual satisfaction in worthwhile accomplishment, recognizes the importance of seeing to it that every bit of work done shall have the *pull of a purpose.*

The author of this book has been a *teacher* in the real sense of the word, as revealed through his ability to create goals or purposes toward which boys have found themselves pulled with as strong a force as the magnet draws the piece of steel to itself. There is no sense in which the book has been produced merely to add another to the thousands which now exist; rather it has come forth from the modesty of its author upon the urge of others who could see the sterling worth of his past work in developing the material which goes to make up the content.

Every boat, airplane and kite included herein has stood the test of actual construction and operation, and has proved to have a strong appeal for boys of junior high school ages. The entire volume, therefore, should be not only a treasure chest for the boy, and an invaluable aid to the teacher in the conduct of classes, but should have still more far-reaching results in showing, through typical concrete example, the way in which real education may be accomplished most effectively.

DEAN M. SCHWEICKHARD.

Assistant Superintendent of City
Schools, Minneapolis, Minnesota

PREFACE

THIS book is intended primarily as a practical work of instruction for the typical American boy who delights in the making of model boats, model airplanes, and kites, be it during his spare time, during the long summer months, or in the school shop during the school year. It is also intended for the manual-arts instructor who includes model boats, model airplanes, and kites as a part of his school program; for the recreation director or leader, on his summer playground program; for the model boat and airplane enthusiasts; and for the aid of Model Clubs.

For many years one feature of shop-work at the Bryant Junior High School, Minneapolis, has been that of model boat building, as a part of the regular instruction in woodwork. Model boat building is one of the most fascinating junior high school problems that one can select. It becomes a simple matter to teach a boy the fundamental processes and related information of your shop course if he is making a model boat that he has long wanted to possess.

Each spring, Bryant Junior High School holds an annual Model Boat Regatta for boys who have constructed boats during the school year.

All model boats included here are the results of many years of experimenting by the author with model boat classes in the junior high school, and with recreation groups on the city playgrounds.

Model boat building and contests have been a part of the Minneapolis Park Board recreation department program for many years. It is a common sight to see a group of boys sailing their much prized model yachts or speeding their model speed boats on some Minneapolis lake almost any day of the spring or summer months.

Kite construction and flying is another handicraft recreational activity conducted by the recreation department of the Minneapolis Park Board during the summer months. At a recent city-wide kite tournament, 1500 kites of various sizes and designs were entered. Kite making may not be considered the best kind of work for the manual-arts shop; but the interest in making kites out of school or in school Clubs, surely can be developed in the school shop by the manual-arts instructor. A kite often serves very well as a supplementary problem in the wood-shop. Kite making is a form of handicraft activity that every boy likes.

Only those kites that have proven the most successful here in our tournaments are illustrated in this small volume.

Model airplane building and flying has been most popular with the boys in this city during the past few years. This kind of work is carried on especially as a Club feature of the Junior High School. As an extracurricular activity or Club feature, model airplane construction and flying is carried on in nearly every junior high school and grade center of the city. At the Bryant Junior High School, as in many other centers, model airplane construction and flying receive their main stimulants from the manual-arts department.

To create as much interest as possible in the construction of model airplanes at the Bryant, several model airplane flying contests are conducted each year in the school auditorium during the winter months. In the spring the young model airplane builders take to the outside models and the great outdoors for their contests.

The art of model airplane building has long been a practical experimental school for aeronautical engineers. All the best known pioneers in airplane development have constructed many models before attempting to build man-sized airplanes.

We find that boys are not only interested in the sport of building model airplanes, but their main interests are really on the modern man-sized cabin planes. It can be said that more than fifty per cent of the boys of today interested in model airplane construction are only expressing their interest in aviation by building model airplanes.

Grateful acknowledgement is made to Dean M. Schweickhard, assistant superintendent of schools, for encouraging model boat, airplane, and kite construction at the Bryant Junior High School, and for his many helpful criticisms and suggestions; to the late J. E. Painter, supervisor of manual training, for helpful suggestions and timely inspiration; to Karl Raymond, director of the recreation department of the Minneapolis Park Board, and to Alice Dietz, assistant director of recreation, for their fine cooperation and the use of kite and model boat program material.

Grateful acknowledgement is made E. J. Hardaker, principal of Bryant Junior High School, for his great untiring interest in boys and girls and their welfare. It is through Mr. Hardaker's fine leadership that model boat building and model airplane activities, like many other boy and girl activities, are made possible at this school.

ARMAND J. LaBERGE.

CONTENTS

PART I

MODEL SAILING-YACHTS AND MODEL MOTOR-BOATS

CHAPTER I

THE "MINNETONKA"—A TWELVE-INCH SAILBOAT

HERE IT IS, BOYS, the boat you have been looking for! It is a regular sailing-yacht, that sails, and has plenty of speed. See Plate I. You can make this boat in your school shop as your first problem in woodwork, or just after you have mastered the steps in squaring stock. There is no reason why you can not make the "Minnetonka" in your own shop or Summer Camp.

Nearly every boy who takes woodwork for the first time at the Bryant Junior High School, Minneapolis, makes one of these sailing crafts.

Of all the projects that I have tried with my boys in beginning woodwork, no problem has been as popular and as well made as the "Minnetonka" 12" yacht.

The "Minnetonka"

Materials Required

(A) Hull, 1 pc, 2"x3¼" x 12½", pine
(B) Keel, 1 pc, ⁹⁄₁₆" x 3¼" x 2", pine
     1 Stove-bolt, ¼" x 4"
(C) Keel-weight, 1 pc, lead, 10 oz.
(D) Deck, 1 pc, ⁵⁄₁₆" x 3¼" x 12¼", red gum or butternut
(E) Mast, 1 pc, ⁵⁄₁₆" x ⁵⁄₁₆" x 17", same
(F) Jib-boom, 1 pc, ¼" x ¼" x 5¼", red gum
(G) Bowsprit, 1 pc, ¼" x ¼" x 3¼", red gum
(H) Gaff, 1 pc, ⁵⁄₁₆" x ⁵⁄₁₆" x 5½", red gum
(I) Boom, 1 pc, ⁵⁄₁₆" x ⁵⁄₁₆" x 10", red gum
(J) Rudder, 1 pc, 1¾" x 2¼", black iron, 28-gage
(K) Rudder-guide, 1 pc, ¾" x 2¼", same

(L) Traveler, 1 pc, wire, 16-gage
(M) Mainsail, 1 pc, 10½" x 13½", muslin
(N) Jib-sail, 1 pc, 5¾" x 13½", muslin
(O) Topsail, 1 pc, 3¾" x 5", muslin
(P) Cleats, 4 pcs, ¼" x ¾", metal
(Q) Deadeyes, 4 pcs, fiber
(U) Mainsail-halyard, fish-line
(V) Back-stay, fish-line
    Rigging, screw-eyes, 1 doz.
        curtain-rings, 2 doz.

Stand

(R) Base, 1 pc, ¾" x 3¼" x 6", red gum **or** butternut
(S) Ends, 2 pcs, ⁵⁄₈" x 2¼" x 4", same
(T) Sides, 2 pcs, ½" x 1" x 3½", same

A group of Bryant Junior High School boys ready for the Annual Regatta

A group of 50 boats of the "Minnetonka" type, on a storage-rack which occupies a minimum of space

THE MINNETONKA

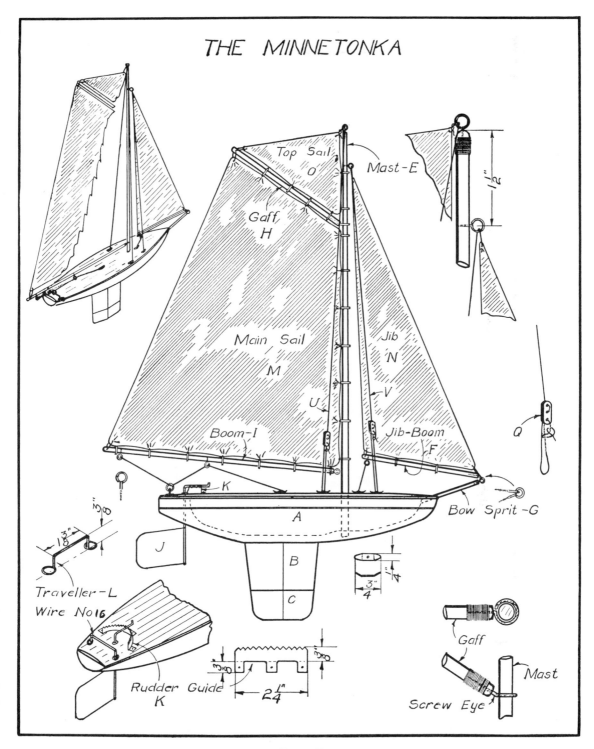

Top Sail
O

Gaff
H

Mast-E

Main Sail
M

Jib
N

V

U

Boom-I

Jib-Boom
F

Q

K

Bow Sprit -G

A

B

C

J

Traveller-L
Wire No 16

Rudder Guide
K

2¼"

Gaff

Mast

Screw Eye

PLATE I

13

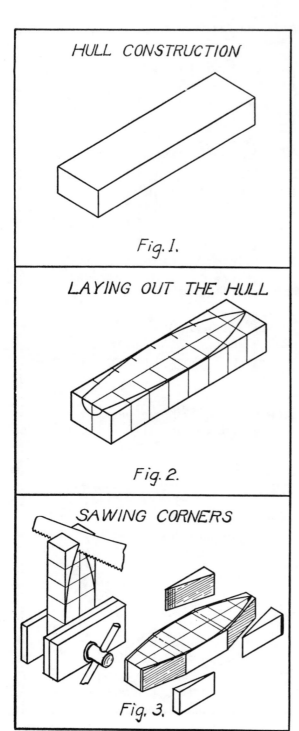

HULL CONSTRUCTION

Fig. 1.

LAYING OUT THE HULL

Fig. 2.

SAWING CORNERS

Fig. 3.

Procedure

The Hull

1. Take a piece of white pine, 2″ x 4¼″ x 12½″, and square it to the finished dimensions, 1¾″ x 3″ x 12″, Fig. 1.

2. Lay out the hull, *A*, according to the detail drawing, Plate II, and Fig. 2.

3. Use a pair of dividers in spacing and measuring on each division line.

4. Saw the corners with a crosscut-saw, as shown in Fig. 3.

5. With a spoke-shave, shape the sides of the boat, as shown in Fig. 4.

6. Saw the bottom next. See Fig. 5.

7. Nail a block to the top of the hull. The hull can then be held in a vise by this block.

8. Shape the outside of the hull, as illustrated in Fig. 6.

9. Make a cradle to hold the hull while carving out the inside, Fig. 7. The corners of your boat can be used for the cradle. The hull can be fastened in the vise without a cradle, but this device makes the work much easier.

10. Gouge the inside of the hull until the walls are ¼″ in thickness, except at the front and back part of the boat. Use a ¾″ or 1″ gouge.

11. Enough space should be left at the back to allow for the rudder.

Wooden Keel

1. Make the wooden keel, *B*, Plate I, by planing a block of pine of the size given in the detail drawing, Plate II, 3¼″ wide at the top and 2¾″ at the bottom, and ⁹⁄₁₆″ thick.

2. Make the keel, *B*, diamond shape next.

3. Bore a ¼″ hole at the exact center of keel, *B*.

SHAPING SIDES

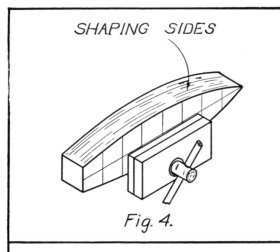

Fig. 4.

SAWING BOTTOM CORNERS

Nail Block

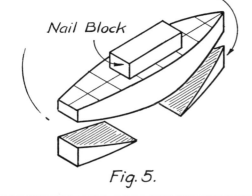

Fig. 5.

SHAPING HULL

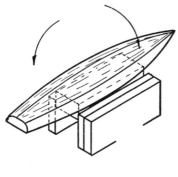

Fig. 6.

GOUGING HULL

Cradle

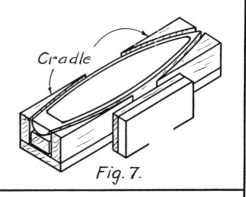

Fig. 7.

FASTEN KEEL

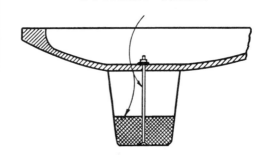

Fig. 8.

FASTEN DECK WITH GLUE AND BRADS.

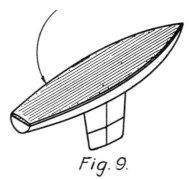

Fig. 9.

Keel-Weight and Mold

1. It will be necessary to make a mold to pour the lead for the keel-weight, *C*.

2. A single mold may be made, like the one shown in the detail drawing, Plate II.

3. However, if several boys are making the boat, much time can be saved by making a series of molds, as shown in Fig. 10.

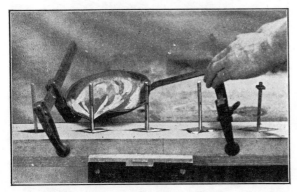

Fig. 10. Pouring lead keels for the Minnetonka." There are ten keels in this mold, of which five are shown.

4. Shellac the inside of the mold, and clamp the three pieces together. The shellac will produce a tight fit, and prevent the lead from leaking through the joints of the mold.

5. A wooden mold of this type can be used at least 50 times, if scraped and shellacked each time.

6. Hold the ¼" x 4" stove-bolt in the center of the mold while pouring the lead.

Fastening Keel to Hull

1. File the lead keel to the proper shape and size, and fasten to the wooden keel, Fig. 8.

2. It is well to shape the two parts of the keel, *B* and *C*, together before attaching to the hull.

3. Fasten the keel to the hull with the ¼" x 4" stove-bolt, and glue. The distance from the back of the boat to the center of the keel bolt is 5⅜".

4. Nail the hull to the keel from the inside also.

The Deck

1. Make the deck according to the shape of the finished hull. Use a wood such as red gum or butternut that finishes nicely in the natural finish.

2. Fasten the deck to the hull with glue and ¾" brads, Fig. 9.

3. Set the brads below the surface of the deck.

4. Round the deck to 1/16" on each side with a block-plane.

5. Fill all nail-holes with a filler or putty the color of the deck, and smooth the surface with No. 0 sandpaper.

6. Bore a 5/16" hole through the deck, 4" from the front of the boat, and part way into the bottom of the boat, to receive the mast. See detail drawing, Plate II.

7. Fig. 11 gives the details of a simple stand on which to mount the ' Minnetonka" when it is out of the water.

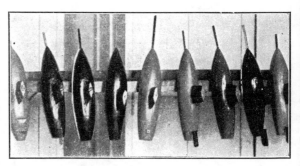

A group of "Minnetonka" boats on the drying-rack

Mast, Booms, Gaff, and Bowsprit

1. Make the mast, *E*, from a piece of red gum or butternut, 5/16" x 5/16" x 7".

2. The shaping of a small stick of this kind is best accomplished by holding the square stick in one hand across the bench

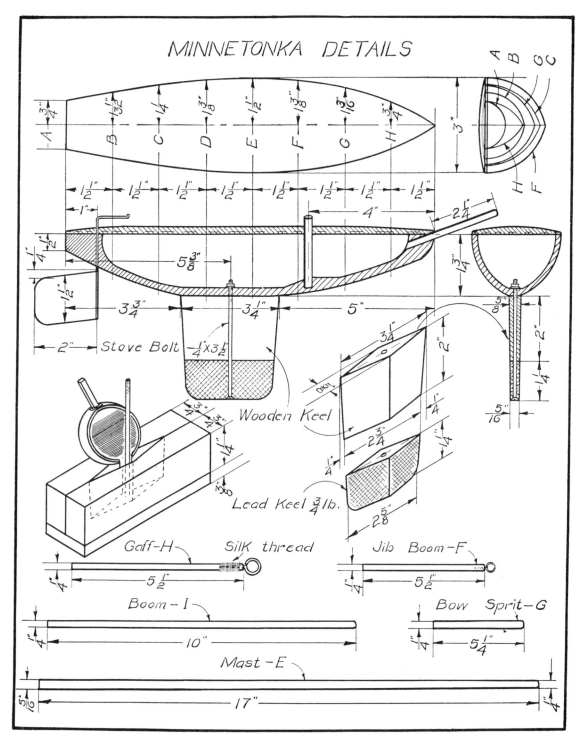

MINNETONKA DETAILS

Stove Bolt — 1/4"x3 1/2"

Wooden Keel

Lead Keel 3/4 lb.

Gaff-H

Silk thread

Jib Boom-F

Boom - I

Bow Sprit-G

Mast - E

PLATE II

17

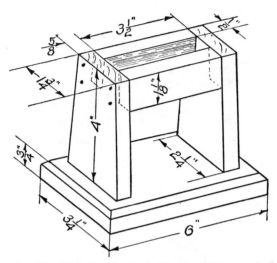

FIG. 11. Details of stand for the "Minnetonka"

while planing with the other hand. Use a block-plane in shaping the mast.

3. The mast can then be made perfectly round by using fine sandpaper.

4. In like manner, the boom, *I*, jib-boom, *F*, gaff, *H*, and bowprit, *G*, can be constructed. See Plate I.

5. Wind silk or fine cotton or linen thread around one end of each of the mast, boom, gaff, and bowsprit. Apply shellac on these parts before winding the thread. The thread will prevent the wood from splitting when inserting the screw-eyes.

6. Glue the mast at the bottom of the boat, as shown in the drawing.

Rudder and Rudder-Guide

1. Make the rudder, *J*, from a piece of black iron, 28-gage.

2. Turn one edge with the wiring machine or a pair of pliers, and solder to a piece of 16-gage wire.

3. Make the rudder-guide, *K*, of black iron, 28-gage, and shape according to drawing.

4. Make the traveler, *L*, out of 16-gage wire.

Finishing

1. A simple gloss paint finish may be used in finishing the "Minnetonka." Lacquer is also very suitable for a project of this type.

2. Give all the parts of the boat one light coat of shellac, and sand with 4-0 sandpaper when dry.

3. Apply one coat of the desired color of paint or lacquer to the hull. Sandpaper with a 4-0 grade of sandpaper when dry.

4. A second or third coat of paint can be used. If the lacquer is used, two coats are usually sufficient.

5. The hull may be finished in two colors: say, white above the water-line and light blue below the water-line.

6. Use a piece of adhesive tape on the water-line for a straight edge, when painting the lower part of the boat.

7. The deck, mast, booms, gaff, and bowsprit should be left in the natural, by using a clear varnish.

Rigging

1. Plate I and Fig. 12 show one simplified type of rigging.

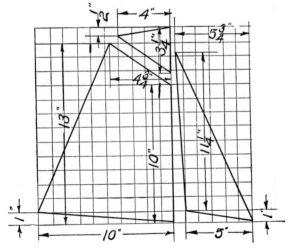

FIG. 12. Sails for the "Minnetonka"

2. Make the sails out of cheese-cloth, muslin, or other light material.

3. Make patterns for the sails out of heavy paper first, Fig. 12.

4. Transfer paper pattern to cloth, allowing for a ¼″ seam.

5. Mother or sister will be only too glad to help on this part of your boat.

6. See Chapter IV, "The Technique of Sailing Model Yachts," for hints on how to sail your boat.

Questions

1. Name the steps in squaring up stock?

2. What is the difference between a crosscut-saw and a rip-saw?

3. How can you tell the size of an auger-bit?

4. What will happen if you put your boat in the water before it has been painted or varnished?

5. Are varnish, paint, lacquer, and shellac waterproof

CHAPTER II

THE "NOKOMIS"—A 26″ SAILING-YACHT

THE "Nokomis" is really a fine sailing-yacht, and can always be depended on to sail in any kind of breeze. See Plate III. It has speed, beautiful lines, and that famous Indian name, *Nokomis,* which makes it that much more interesting. Lake Harriet in Minneapolis, which is approximately three-quarters of a mile in width, is our testing place for model yachts of the "Nokomis" type, Fig. 13. This model can speed across the lake and back in very good time. It will also perform well on a smaller body of water.

If the following directions and drawings are followed, you cannot help but have one of the best sailing-yachts in your community. Try it and see.

This model is a very popular project in my second-term woodworking classes—8B and 8A grade pupils.

The "Nokomis"

FIG. 13.   The "Nokomis," winner of an Annual Regatta Race in the 26″ Yacht Class.   This photograph
shows the position of sails and boat as the boat came in to shore

Materials Required

(A)   Hull, 1 pc, 3¼″ x 6½″ x 26″, bass or pine
(B)   Deck, 1 pc, ⁵⁄₁₆″ x 6½″ x 26″, red gum or mahogany
(C)   Keel, 1 pc, 7½″ x 12¾″, black iron, 20-gage
(D)   Keel-weight, 1 pc, 2½ lbs.
(E)   Mast, 1 pc, ½″ x ½″ x 36″, red gum
(F)   Jib-boom, 1 pc, ⁵⁄₁₆″ x ⁵⁄₁₆″ x 10½″, red gum
(G)   Boom, 1 pc, ⁵⁄₁₆″ x ⁵⁄₁₆″ x 20½″, red gum
(H)   Bowsprit, 1 pc, ⅜″ x ⅜″ x 8″, red gum
(I)   Rudder, 1 pc, 3¼″ x 4⅞″, black iron, 26-gage
(J)   Tiller, 1 pc, ¼″ x 4″, brass, 20 gage
(K)   Mainsail, 1 pc, 21″ x 31″, long-cloth, or lonsdale cambric
(L)   Jib-sail, 1 pc, 13″ x 23″, same
(O)   Mainsail-halyard, fish-line

(P)   Rudder-rod, 1 pc, ⅛″ diameter x 4½″ long, brass rod
(Q)   Rudder-port, 1 pc, ³⁄₁₆″ diameter x 2⅜″ long, brass tubing
(R)   Jib-halyard, fish-line
(S)   Mainsail-halyard, fish-line
        Screw-eyes, 1 doz.
        Curtain-rings, 1 doz., ⅝″ diameter

Cabin

Sides, 2 pcs, ³⁄₁₆″ x ⅞″ x 8″, red gum or butternut
Top, 1 pc, ¼″ x 3″ x 6″, same

Stand

Sides, 2 pcs, ¾″ x 7″ x 8½″, butternut
Bottom, 1 pc, ¾″ x 5″ x 8″, butternut
Braces, 2 pcs, ¾″ x 1¼″ x 4½″, butternut

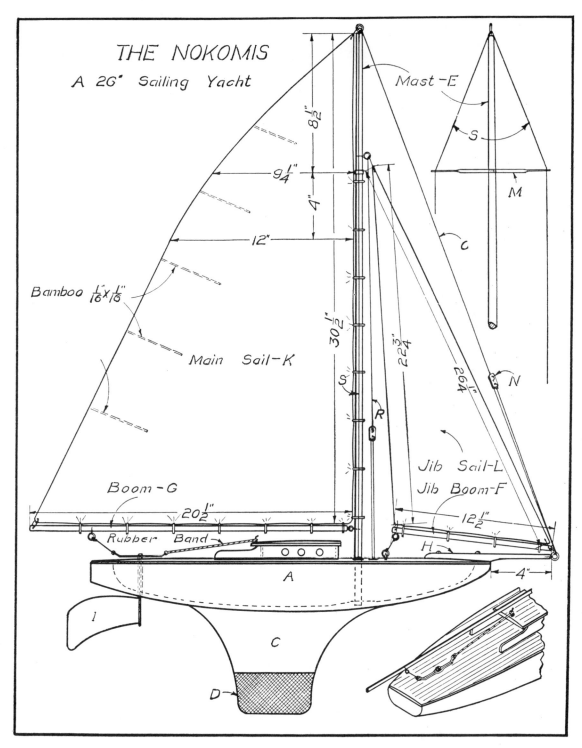

THE NOKOMIS

A 26" Sailing Yacht

Mast – E

Bamboo $\frac{1}{16}$" x $\frac{1}{16}$"

Main Sail – K

Boom – G

Rubber Band

Jib Sail – L

Jib Boom – F

PLATE III

21

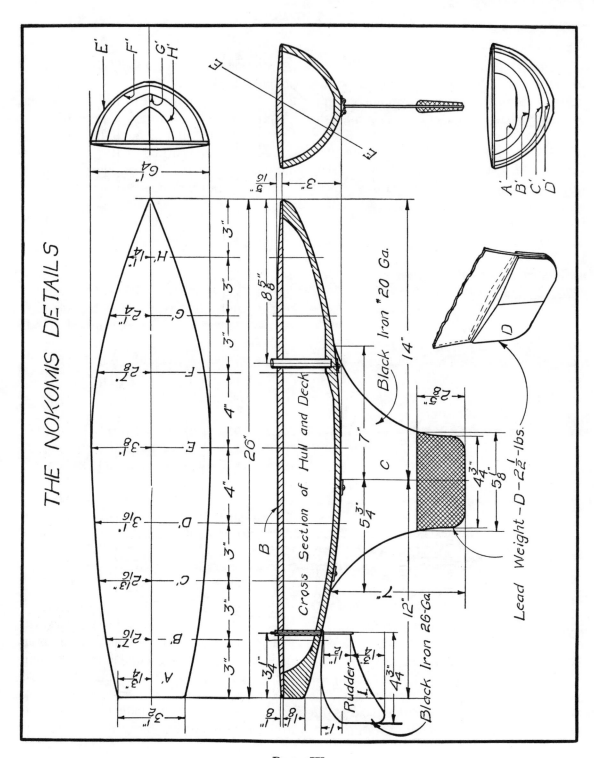

THE NOKOMIS DETAILS

Cross Section of Hull and Deck

Black Iron "20 Ga.

Black Iron 26-Ga.

Rudder

Lead Weight – D – 2½ lbs.

PLATE IV

22

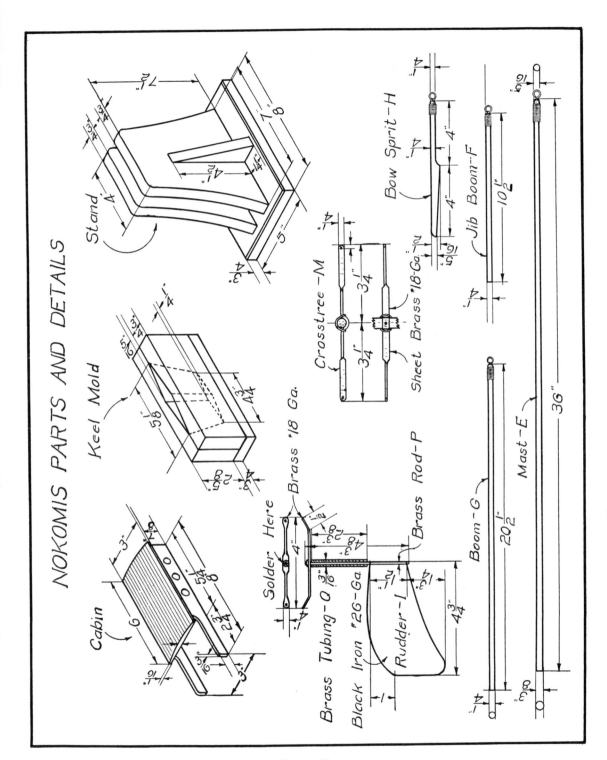

NOKOMIS PARTS AND DETAILS

PLATE V

23

FIG. 14. Gouging out the inside of the hull, while it is held in the vise by means of a cradle

Procedure

The Hull

1. Select a good solid block of pine or bass for the hull and plane to 3″ in thickness.

2. If a good solid block cannot be found, build up the hull from 1″ or 2″ boards. Use the best of glue that is water-proof, and leave your hull in the clamps at least 24 hours.

3. Lay out the hull, A, according to the detail drawing, Plate IV.

4. Use a pair of dividers and rule in spacing and measuring on each of the division lines, A; B; C; etc.

5. Saw the corners with a crosscut-saw or turning-saw, as shown in Fig. 3.

6. Shape the sides of the hull next. See Fig. 4.

7. Saw the bottom corners. See Fig. 5.

8. Nail a block to the top of the hull, as shown in Fig. 5. The hull can then be held securely in the vise while shaping the under part of the hull.

9. Shape the outside of the hull, as illustrated in Fig. 6, and detail drawing, Plate IV. This is the most important part of your boat, and care and good judgement should be used in performing this job. Take your time, and keep at it until you are satisfied that your hull is well balanced and well shaped. An accurate eye is the best judge while shaping the hull.

10. Templates can be used at different points, if one wishes the most accurate of jobs.

11. With a 1″ gouge, gouge out the inside of the hull until the walls are ¼″ in thickness, except at the front and back of the boat. See detail drawing, Plate IV, and Fig. 14.

12. Make the inside of the hull as smooth as possible with sandpaper, and apply a coat of white lead.

The Deck

1. Make the deck from a wood that finishes up nicely in the natural, such as red gum, mahogany, or walnut.

2. Shape the deck according to the shape of the finished hull.

3. Give the under part of the deck a coat of white lead, and fasten the deck to the hull with glue and ⅞″ brads.

4. Set the nails below the surface of the wood.

5. Shape the top of the deck to ⅛″ in thickness on the sides. This can best be done with a smooth-plane or block-plane. See cross-section drawing, Plate IV.

6. Fill all nail-holes with filler the color of the deck. Fine sandpaper dust with glue makes a good filler for nail-holes.

7. Bore a ⅜″ hole at a center point of the deck, 8⅝″ from the front of the boat, to receive the mast. Bore also part way into the bottom of the boat, as shown in the detail drawing.

Mast, Booms, and Bowsprit

1. Make the mast, E, from a piece of red gum, ½″ x ½″ x 36″. Scribe circles on each end of the mast. The mast should be ⅜″ in diameter at the bottom, and 5⁄16″ in diameter at the top.

2. The shaping of the mast can be done by holding the square stick in one hand across the bench while planing with the other hand. The mast can also be clamped in the vise if necessary.

3. Use a block-plane or a jack-plane in shaping the mast.

4. The mast can then be made perfectly round by using fine sandpaper.

5. In like manner, the booms, F, G, and the bowsprit, H, can be constructed.

6. Wind silk or fine thread around the end of the mast and around one end of each of the booms and bowsprit. Apply shellac on these parts before winding the thread. The thread will prevent the wood from splitting when inserting the screw-eyes.

The Keel

1. Make the keel, C, from black iron, 20-gage. Shape it according to detail drawing, Plate IV.

2. Turn the top edge into ½″ flanges on each side of the keel, as shown.

3. Drill a 3⁄16″ hole in each flange.

Keel-Weight and Mold

1. It will be necessary to make a mold to receive the molten lead for the keel-weight.

2. Make a single mold according to the detail drawing, Plate V.

3. Shellac the inside part of the mold pieces and clamp together. The shellac will produce a tight fit and prevent the lead from leaking through. A mold of this type can be used many times if scraped and shellacked each time.

4. Hold the metal keel in the mold while pouring the lead.

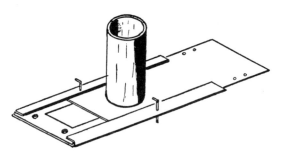

FIG. 15. Details of the sliding mast-step, made of sheet-metal, 1″ wide, by 2¼″ long

Fastening Mast and Keel

1. Glue the mast at the bottom of the hull and deck, as illustrated in the detail drawing, Plate IV.

2. I find that a boy has less trouble with his boat if the mast is stationary, and glued solid at the point shown in the drawing. The locating of the mast at this point has been the result of my experience with hundreds of model yachts of the "Nokomis" type during the past twelve years.

3. However, if one wishes, a mast-step or strut may be used, Fig. 15. Two deck-beams will be necessary if a mast-step is used.

4. File the lead keel-weight, *D*, to the proper shape and weight, and fasten to the hull with $\frac{3}{8}''$ x 6, R-H screws.

5. Make sure that your lead weight does not weigh more than $2\frac{1}{2}$ pounds.

6. Locate the center of your boat, and place the keel 12" from the stern of the hull to the center of the keel.

7. Fasten the bowsprit to the deck with $\frac{3}{4}''$ x 6, R-H screws. Bore holes in the bowsprit before inserting the screws.

Rudder

1. Make the rudder, *I*, from a piece of black iron, $3\frac{1}{4}''$ x 5", 26-gage.

2. Make it the shape illustrated in the detail drawing, Plate V, and turn the small edge to receive the rudder-rod, *P*.

3. Turn the edge with a pair of pliers or the wiring-machine.

4. Solder the rudder to a piece of brass rod, $\frac{1}{8}''$ in diameter by $4\frac{3}{8}''$ in length.

5. Bore a $\frac{3}{16}''$ hole $3\frac{1}{4}''$ from the stern of the boat at a center point for the rudder-port, *Q*.

6. Make the tiller, *J*, from sheet brass, 18-gage, as shown in the detail drawing.

7. Make the rudder-port, *Q*, from $\frac{3}{16}''$ brass tubing. Cement the port to the deck and to the bottom of the hull. Ship cement will make the port solid and waterproof.

8. Insert the brass rod part of the rudder in the port, *Q*, and solder the tiller to the top of it.

Finishing

1. For the finishing turn to Chapter V, "Methods of Finishing Model Boats."

Rigging and Sails

1. Plate III shows a very popular type of sails for model yachts, known as the "Marconi Rig."

2. Make the sails from lonsdale cambric or long-cloth.

3. Make patterns for the sails out of heavy paper first. Consult the drawing for dimensions.

4. Transfer your paper pattern to the cloth, allowing for a $\frac{3}{8}''$ seam, and cut on the line.

5. Mother or sister will be only too glad to help on this part of your boat.

6. Sew the curtain-rings to the sails, and fit the sails to the rigging.

7. See Chapter IV, "The Technique of Sailing Model Yachts," for points on how to sail your boat.

Questions

1. How do you sharpen a gouge

2. What other method of hull construction can you name?

3. Why is a keel necessary on a model yacht

4. How much can you build the "Nokomis" for?

5. Is inside varnish satisfactory in finishing a model boat?

CHAPTER III

THE "MINNEHAHA"—A 38" SAILING-YACHT

WHEN you build the "Minnehaha," Boys, and enter your sailing-yacht in a contest, you can imagine that you are guiding the famous "Interprize" to victory. You may remember the America's Cup yacht race, in which Harold Vanderbilt and his famous "Interprize" outmaneuvered and outdistanced Sir Thomas Lipton and his great yacht, the "Shamrock," in a series of races.

The "Minnehaha" is really a great model yacht, and is sure to give you many hours of thrills and good time. See Fig. 16 and Plate VI. It does, however, require time and accurate workmanship in order to produce a good model. But who minds a little extra time and a bit more care, if he knows he can produce a sailing-yacht of his own liking?

This yacht can be built in your own school shop in the 8A or 9B grade, or you can build it in your own home shop during your leisure hours.

Many of these 38" sailing-yachts have been constructed in my 9B classes during the past several years.

The "Minnehaha"

Materials Required

(A) Hull, 1 pc, 4" x 8¼" x 38", pine or bass
(B) Deck, 1 pc, ½" x 8¼" x 38", red gum or mahogany
(C) Keel, 1 pc, ⅞" x 13" x 5", pine
(D) Keel-weight, 1 pc, lead, 5 lbs.
    Machine-bolt, 1, ¼" x 9½"
(E) Mast, 1 pc, ⅝" x ⅝" x 50", red gum or pine
(F) Boom, 1 pc, ½" x ½" x 29", same

(G) Main jib-boom, 1 pc, ⅜" x ⅜" x 11", same
(H) Fore jib-boom, 1 pc, ⅜" x ⅜" x 10", same
(I) Bowsprit, 1 pc, ¾" x ¾" x 12", same
(J) Rudder, 1 pc, 5½" x 7", black iron, 26-gage
(K) Mainsail, 1 pc, 30" x 42", long-cloth, or lonsdale cambric
(L) Main jib-sail, 1 pc, 10½" x 42", same
(M) Fore jib-sail, 1 pc, 9½" x 42", same
    Screw-eyes, 1 doz.; 6 medium, 6 small
    Curtain-rings, 2 doz., ⅝" diameter
(O) Gaff, 1 pc, ¾" x 1¼" x 22", red gum or pine
(P) Rudder port, 1 pc, ¼" diameter x 4¾", brass tubing
(Q) Rudder-rod, 1 pc, 3/16" diameter x 11½", brass rod
    Brass nuts, 2, to fit rudder-rod
(R) Tiller, 1 pc, ¼" x 5½", brass, 18-gage
(S) Mainsail-halyard, fish-line

(*T*) Jib-halyard, fish-line
(*U*) Stays, wire
(*V*) Traveler, 1 pc, copper wire, 16-gage

Mold

Sides, 2 pcs, ¾″ x 3¾″ x 12″, pine or birch
Bottom, 1 pc, ¾″ x 2″ x 12″, same

Stand

Sides, 2 pcs, ¾″ x 9″ x 8½″, butternut or red gum
Bottom, 1 pc, ¾″ x 6½″ x 10½″, same
Braces, 2 pcs, ¾″ x 1¼″ x 6½″, same

FIG. 16. "The Minnehaha" (right), and the "Minnetonka," ready for the races

Procedure

1. Select a good solid block of bass or pine, and plane it to 3¾″ in thickness.

2. If a good solid block cannot be secured, build up the hull from boards or planks 1″ or 2″ in thickness.

3. Use a good grade of glue, that is water-proof, to glue up the hull. Leave the glued up hull in the clamps for at least 24 hours.

4. Lay out the hull, *A*, according to the detail drawing, Plate VII.

5. Use a pair of dividers and rule in spacing and measuring on each division line A, B, C, etc.

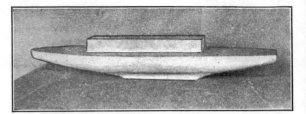

FIG. 17. Hull of the 38″ Model Sailboat

6. Saw the corners with a turning-saw, jig-saw, or band-saw. See Fig. 3.

7. Shape the sides of the hull next, as shown in Fig. 4.

8. Saw the bottom corners similar to Fig. 5. See details of the "Minnehaha," Plates VII and VIII.

9. Nail a solid block to the top of the hull, as illustrated in Fig. 5, Fig. 6 and Fig. 17. The hull can be held securely in the vise by this block while shaping the outside of the hull.

10. The shaping of the under part of the hull is the most important part of your yacht. Study the drawing and cross-sections shown in Plate VII, carefully before starting on the job.

FIG. 18. Shaping the hull of the "Minnehaha"

11. Start shaping the outside of the hull, *A*, as shown in Fig. 6. Use the drawknife, jack-plane, and spoke-shave in doing this job.

12. Use a 1″ gouge to shape the concave curve toward the keel, as shown in Fig.

THE MINNEHAHA

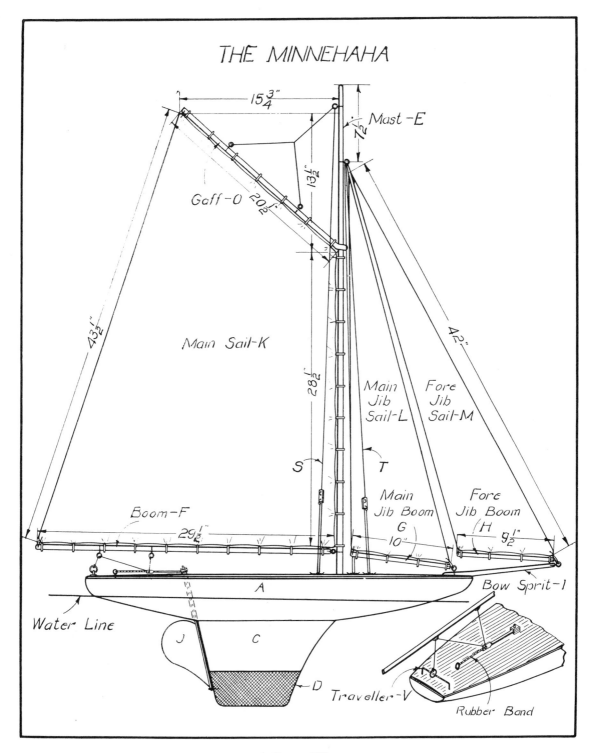

PLATE VI

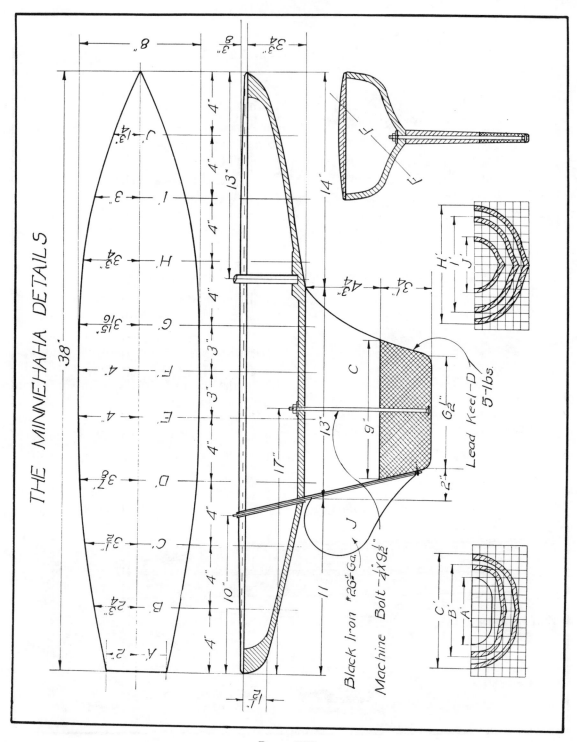

THE MINNEHAHA DETAILS

PLATE VII

30

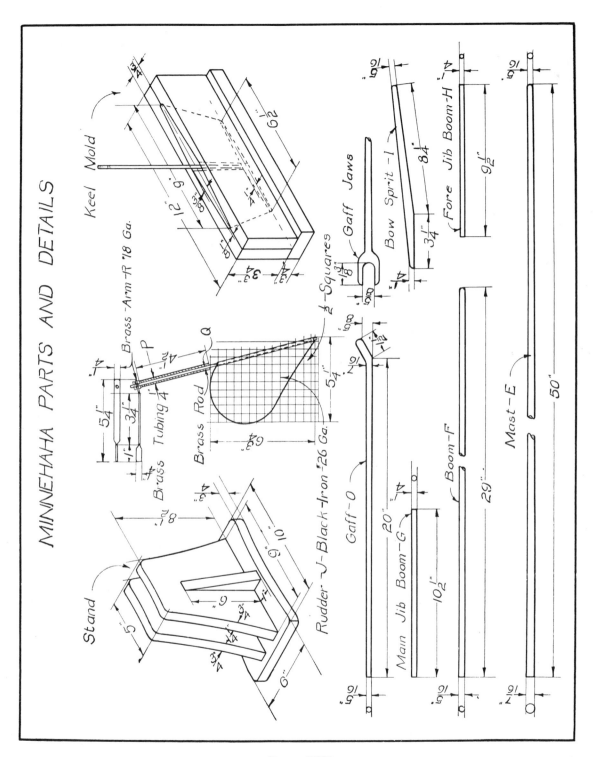

MINNEHAHA PARTS AND DETAILS

PLATE VIII

31

18. Take your time and keep at the task until the hull is well balanced and well shaped. A trained eye is the best judge while performing this job.

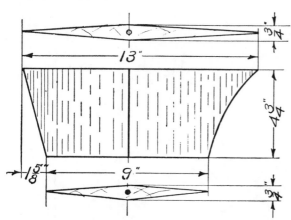

FIG. 19. Details of the wooden keel, C, of the "Minnehaha"

13. It is well to cut from cardboard or sheet-metal, templates which correspond to each cross-section as shown in Plate VII. Check your hull with these patterns as you progress with the shaping of the hull.

14. Make a cradle to hold the hull while carving the inside part of the hull. See Fig. 14 and Fig. 7.

15. With a 1" gouge and a mallet, gouge out the inside of the hull until the walls are 1/4" in thickness or less, except at the bow and stern of the boat. The bottom should be left over 1/4" in thickness, especially at the point where the mast is to be placed.

16. Make the inside of the hull as smooth as possible with sandpaper.

17. Apply a heavy coat of paint to the inside of your hull.

Wooden Keel

1. Make the wooden keel, C, by planing a piece of white pine to the size and shape shown in Fig. 19. The keel should be 13" wide at the top, 9½" in width at the bottom, and ¾" in thickness.

2. Note that the keel is straight on the back part, Fig. 20.

3. Make the keel diamond shape first.

4. Bore a 1/4" hole that is at the exact center of the keel, transversely, and that is at the center of the lower part of the keel, longitudinally.

Keel-Weight and Mold

1. It will be necessary to make a mold in order to pour the lead for the keel-weight, D. See the detail drawing, Plate VIII.

2. Shellac the inside part of the mold pieces, and clamp them together.

3. Hold the 1/4" machine-bolt at the exact center of your mold while pouring the molten lead. See Fig. 21 and Fig. 22.

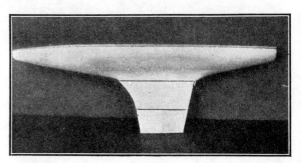

FIG. 20

Fastening Keel to Hull

1. File the lead keel, D, to the proper shape and size, and fasten to the wood keel, C. It is well to shape the two parts of the keel (C and D) together before attaching to the hull. Care should be taken in filing the keel to a fin-like shape. Make it as thin through the center as possible.

2. Make sure that your lead weight, D, does not weigh more than five pounds.

FIG. 21.   Pouring the lead for the keel-weight

FIG. 22.   The keel-weight with front half of mold removed, after pouring

3. Bore a ¼" hole through the bottom of the hull, at a center point and 17" from the stern or back of the boat, Plate VII.

4. Attach the keel to the hull, *A*, with the ¼" machine-bolt and glue. Make sure that the bolt is perfectly tight.

5. Nail the hull to the wooden keel, *C*, from the inside with 1¾" nails, also.

The Deck

1. The deck for the "Minnehaha" can be made from mahogany, walnut, or red gum. The above woods finish up very nicely in the natural color of the wood. Shape the deck from a piece of wood, ½" x 8¼" x 38", according to the top shape of the hull.

2. Give the under part of the deck a heavy coat of paint, and fasten the deck to the hull with glue and 1" brads. Set the heads of the brads below the surface of the wood.

3. The raised deck should have a curved top from ⅜" at the center to ⅛" to the sides. This can best be accomplished by planing the top part of the deck with a block-plane or smoothing-plane while the boat is held in a vise.

4. Bore a ⁷⁄₁₆" hole at the center point of the deck, 13" from the front of the boat. Bore also part way in to the bottom of the boat to receive the mast, as shown in the detail drawing, Plate VII.

5. Fill all nail-holes with filler the color of the wood.

Mast, Booms, Bowsprit, and Gaff

1. Make the mast, *E*, from a piece of pine, or red gum, ⅝" x ⅝" x 50". Make a circle of the size required on each end of the mast. The mast should be ⁷⁄₁₆" in diameter at the lower end, slanting to ⁵⁄₁₆" at the top, Plate VIII.

2. The shaping of the mast can be done by holding the square stock in one hand across the bench while planing with the other hand, using a block-plane or jack-plane. The mast can gradually be made round in this manner. Use fine sandpaper to get it perfectly round.

3. In like manner, the booms, *F*, *G*, and bowsprit, *I*, can be constructed.

4. The gaff, *O,* is also made like the mast with a plane, except around the jaws which can be finished with a sloyd-knife or pocket-knife.

5. Wind silk or fine thread around one end of each of the mast, booms, and bow-sprit. Apply shellac on these parts before winding the thread. The thread tightly wound around these places will prevent the wood from splitting when inserting the screw-eyes.

6. Glue the mast at the bottom of the hull and deck, as illustrated in the detail drawing, Plate VII. The locating of the mast at this particular point and gluing it solid have been the results of my experience with a great many model yachts of the "Minnehaha" type during the past several years.

7. If you wish to use a mast-step on top of the deck, refer to Fig. 15.

Rudder

1. Make the rudder, *J,* from a piece of black iron, 5½" x 7", 26-gage.

2. Make it of the shape suggested in the drawing, Plate VIII, and turn the straight edge to receive the rudder-rod, *Q.* Turn the edge with a pair of pliers or the wiring-machine.

3. Solder the rudder to a piece of brass rod, ³⁄₁₆" in diameter. Thread the top end of rod, *Q.*

4. Bore a ¼" hole 10" from the stern of the boat at a center point for the rudder-port. Bore so the hole will hit directly back of the keel, Plate VII.

5. Make the tiller, *R,* from sheet-brass, 18-gage as shown in Plate VIII.

6. Make the rudder-port, *P,* from ¼" brass tubing.

7. After the port, *P,* has been inserted in its proper place, open the tube a little on each end by tapping lightly with a nail-set and hammer. Ship cement can also be used around the tube to prevent the water from leaking into the hull.

8. Insert the brass rod part of the rudder in the port, *P.* Lock the tiller to the rudder-rod with two brass nuts.

9. The lower part of the rudder may be inserted in the lead or fastened to the keel with fine wire.

Boat-Stand

1. Your boat is not complete unless it has a dry-dock or boat-stand to rest on while it is being finished or not sailing on the water. See detail drawing, Plate VIII.

2. This stand can be made from butter-nut, red gum, or oak, any one of which finishes up nicely in the natural color.

3. The stand is assembled with flat-head screws and nails.

Finishing

1. For the finishing of the "Minnehaha," turn to Chapter V, "Methods of Finishing Model Boats."

Questions

1. What is meant by the term, *starboard?*

2. What is meant by the term, *aweather?*

3. What is meant by the term, *trim sails?*

4. What is meant by the term, *tack?*

5. What are *stays?*

CHAPTER IV

THE TECHNIQUE OF SAILING MODEL YACHTS

ONE MAY think that sailing a model yacht the way you want it to sail is a very simple matter. But the sailing of a model yacht is considered an art, and practice and patience are necessary to obtain the best results. Experimental adjustments of the sails and spars are essential to success in the sailing of your particular boat. I suggest that you familiarize yourself with the yachting terms given at the end of this Chapter.

The following are a few suggestions on how to make your yacht go.

Trim Sails.—In a model yacht the sails are *trimmed;* or, in other words, they are set so that the boat will continue to sail along a course decided upon by the young sailor.

The idea of holding a straight course is to get your boat across a given distance as speedily as possible.

The trim of the sails will depend upon the wind.

Aweather, or Scudding.—Aweather or scudding means sailing toward the direction of the wind.

When scudding or sailing with the wind, the sails behind the foremast should be slackened out as far as they will go. This will move the booms almost at right angles with the center-line of the boat.

A model boat will sail fairly well with the wind, but you do not always get the best speed aweather.

Steering is difficult when running with the wind, especially in rough water. There is danger of the sails getting in the water.

Reaching.—Sailing with the wind sideways is called "reaching."

If the boat is sailing with the wind blowing midway between one of the sides and the stern, across the deck, it is called "three-quarter sailing." This type of sailing is very effective.

A model yacht will continue a great distance at top speed on a reach while scudding.

The jib-sails should be pulled fairly tight, while the backsail or mainsail should be made slack. The mainsail should, however, not be so slack as when sailing with the wind.

The sails may be slackened or tightened, depending on the angle at which the wind is striking the boat.

When sailing a new boat, the best trim for different points of sailing can be found only by experiment.

Beating to Windward.—If you wish your model to sail against the wind, this is called "beating to windward." To sail directly against the wind is almost impossible, but a boat will move against a wind blowing at a very small angle on her bowsprit.

As soon as a model reaches the limit of her course or the shore, the young sailor can turn her bow on a small angle, so as to bring the wind on the opposite side of the boat; and, in this way, a second lap of the trip is started.

Tacking.—These zigzag runs or laps are known as "tacking," and are repeated until the model yacht arrives at the end of her trip or destination.

Tacking is very slow work, and a great distance must be traveled before a definite place can be reached. Tacking with a model yacht is a lot of fun, and gives a fellow plenty of good experience.

Tacking is the only way you can sail your model yacht in a direction against the wind.

YACHTING TERMS DEFINED FOR MODEL YACHT BUILDERS

Abaft. Behind, toward the stern.

Abeam. At right angles to the side and in horizontal plane.

Aweather. Toward the direction of the wind.

Beam. The widest part of a vessel.

Boom. The lower spar for a fore-and-aft sail

Bow. Sides of the front part of the boat. The right hand is the *starboard* bow; and the left hand, the *port* bow.

Hull. The entire structure of a ship outside of the equipment.

Jib. Triangular sail set forward of the foremast.

Keel. The principal timber in a ship or boat, usually extending from stem to stern at the bottom, and supporting the framework.

Leeward. The side opposite to that from which the wind is blowing.

Leeway. The amount a vessel is carried to leeward by the wind.

List. When one side of a boat lies deeper in the water than the other, caused by a shifting of the load.

Mast. A long, round piece of timber standing upright in a vessel, and supporting the yards, sails, and rigging in general.

Midships. Middle part of a ship.

Port. The left side of a vessel, looking forward.

Reach. A long tack with wind abeam.

Rigging. The entire equipment of a ship, masts, spars, ropes, etc.

Rudder. A device for steering the boat, fastened to the outside of the hull, usually at the stern.

Sail. A piece of cloth or other fabric to catch the wind, and so to carry the boat through the water.

Sloop. A boat with one mast, having a jib-sail.

Spinnaker. A racing sail shaped like a jib-sail.

Spar. A piece of wood of any shape used as a mast, bowsprit, yard, etc.

Starboard. The right side of a vessel, looking forward.

Stern. The back part of a boat.

Stays. Wire ropes which brace a mast from forward.

Tack. To change the direction of sailing due to the wind.

Trim sails. To set the sails properly.

Water-line. Submerging line of a ship, with or without cargo.

CHAPTER V

METHODS OF FINISHING MODEL BOATS

YOU MIGHT make the best model sail-boat or motor-boat in the world, but if the finish is poorly done, your good work will seem in vain. You should spend a lot of time in finishing your model boat. Make it the most important job on your boat. A good finish can be put on to suit your taste as to color, as well as to pre-serve the wood of your good ship against weather conditions.

In this Chapter, four methods of finishing model boats are described: (1) finishing with paint and enamel; (2) finishing in the natural color, with spar-varnish; (3) finishing with lacquer; and (4) finishing with filler, stain, and varnish.

I. FINISHING WITH PAINT AND ENAMEL

1. Do the finishing in a dry room (70° F.).

2. Prepare the surface of the hull carefully.

3. Check the surface, and make sure that all tool-marks, chipped grain, and surplus glue are entirely removed.

4. Sand the boat first with No. 0 sand-paper, and finish with No. 4-0 sandpaper.

5. Dust off the hull carefully, so it will be absolutely free of dust before painting.

6. Use a ready-mixed paint for the undercoats. If you choose the ready-mixed paint, thin it down to the consistency of cream. Add a few drops of Japan dryer to a half-pint of paint.

7. The best paint for water protection, however, is pure white lead mixed in the following proportions. Dissolve four parts of white lead to one part of dryer with turpentine; add a few drops of linseed-oil to make the lead work freely.

8. Apply three or four coats of the ready-mixed paint or white lead, rubbing each coat down with No. 4-0 sandpaper. Each coat should be allowed to dry at least 24 hours before sanding.

APPLYING THE ENAMEL

1. Make sure the surface of your hull is absolutely smooth and free of dust before applying the enamel.

2. Enamel is more expensive than paint for the final finish, but it makes a very desirable finish for model boats, due to its wearing qualities and fine appearance. Enamel may be purchased in small quantities on the market in almost any color.

A light blue for the lower part of the boat, and white above the water-line, present a very good combination.

3. Apply a first coat of enamel with a good brush. A camel's-hair brush, 1″ or 1½″ in width, works very well.

4. Flow and brush this first coat on evenly. If you decide on finishing the lower part of your boat in blue, give the entire hull a coat of blue.

5. Allow the enamel to dry for at least 48 hours, unless it is a quick-drying enamel.

6. When dry, remove all gloss and rough spots with No. 4-0 sandpaper, by sanding very lightly. Be careful not to rub through the enamel.

7. Dust off the surface thoroughly, and apply a second coat of enamel as it comes from the container.

8. Be very careful with this second coat of enamel; flow it on very evenly; and let it dry thoroughly before proceeding with the rubbing.

9. The next step will be to find out how deep in the water the boat will float. In case of the motor boat, load the boat with necessary batteries and motor; and, in case of the sailboat, attach the deck and spars in their respective places.

10. When the water and the boat are perfectly still, sprinkle some powdered charcoal on each side of the boat in the water. This charcoal will stick to the sides of your boat and mark clearly the water-line.

11. Take the boat out of the water, and with a soft pencil and a straight edge mark a light line in the charcoal line.

12. A small ⅛″ reed split in two makes a good water-line. See the 38″ Motor-Boat, Model A, page 55. The reed is attached to the boat with glue and a few brads. It is best to finish the reed the desired color before it is attached to your boat. A dark blue will show off very well, if the lower part of the boat is painted light blue and the upper part white.

13. After you have located the water-line, apply one or two coats of white enamel or a color of your own choice above the water-line, rubbing between coats with No. 4-0 sandpaper.

14. If you prefer to paint a narrow strip ¼″ or ⅜″ in width for the water-line, it should be done before the final rub down is given the hull.

15. Use a small flat striping brush for this job.

16. With fine pumice-stone and oil, rub and polish the outside of your hull to a high polish and lustre.

II. FINISHING IN THE NATURAL COLOR OF THE WOOD

1. It is very difficult to find a stain that will produce a better color than the natural color of a beautiful red mahogany, dark walnut, red gum, or even a dark brown butternut wood. If any of the above-mentioned woods are available in your community, by all means use them and finish them in the natural colors.

2. Apply a thin coat of white shellac to your deck, cabin, and spars, as an undercoat, or as a filler for the varnish.

3. Sand the white shellac lightly with the grain, with No. 4-0 sandpaper. Dust off the surface clean before applying the varnish.

APPLYING SPAR-VARNISH

Spar-varnish was first used for varnishing the spars and other outer parts of ships exposed to the varied weather conditions. It is considered the best kind of varnish for outside work, especially model boats. Spar-varnish contains a large proportion of oil, to make it tough, and a high grade of varnish-gum, to make it lasting.

1. Use the varnish as it comes from the container, and apply in a room with a temperature of 70° F., or above.

2. Use a 1″ varnish-brush, and flow the varnish on, covering the deck and other

parts well. Be careful that the varnish does not run on the sides.

3. Do not brush when the varnish becomes sticky.

4. Allow this first coat at least 48 hours to dry. In damp weather, the varnish will take more time to dry.

5. In order to produce a good finish with varnish, the varnish should be rubbed down between coats. The object of rubbing is to improve the appearance by removing possible rough spots.

6. Sand this first coat of varnish with No. 4-0 sandpaper very lightly. Sand with the grain, using very light pressure. Be careful not to sand through the varnish.

7. Clean all surfaces free of dust before applying a second coat.

8. Apply a second coat of clear varnish in the same manner as the first coat, and allow this coat to dry 48 hours or more.

9. When perfectly dry, rub this second coat with fine pumice-stone and water. Use a piece of felt to polish the varnish. Rub with the grain.

10. Wipe the surfaces clean and dry with a soft cloth when the polishing is done. The surfaces of all parts must be absolutely clean before a final and third coat of varnish is applied.

11. Apply a third and final coat of spar-varnish to your deck, cabin, and spars.

12. For the best results, allow the varnish to dry for a couple of days or more before polishing this coat.

13. To get a really good finish, rub the varnish with fine pumice-stone and water. Use a felt pad to rub with.

14. Rottenstone may be used next to produce a better finish. Rottenstone is a brown shale which has been ground to a very fine powder. It is softer than pumice, and produces a finer and higher polish.

15. Rub the surfaces with rottenstone and oil, using a soft felt pad until a high polish has been obtained. The rubbing with the rottenstone should remove any possible scratches caused by pumice or fine sandpaper.

III. FINISHING WITH LACQUER

A lacquer finish is a very desirable and popular finish to apply to a model boat. There are many lacquers on the market that can be successfully applied with a brush. Lacquer can be compared very favorably with varnish. Lacquer is waterproof, and is not affected by different weather conditions. It does not crack and check as easily as varnish. Lacquer dries rapidly, and produces a very fine luster.

1. Prepare the surface for the lacquer by applying one or two thin coats of white shellac.

2. Sand the shellac with No. 4-0 sandpaper between coats.

3. Apply, or flow on, the desired color of lacquer with a good brush. Do not brush over the same place more than once. Lacquer cannot be brushed back and forth like paint, and therefore must be applied on very quickly.

4. Sand lightly with No. 4/0 sandpaper when dry, and wipe surface free of dust.

5. Flow on a second coat of lacquer very carefully and evenly.

6. After you have applied two coats of lacquer to the entire hull, find the water-line. See page 38 for directions for finding the water-line.

7. If you desire to finish your boat in

two colors, flow on a coat of black or white lacquer above the water-line, or a color of your own choice.

8. Sand this coat lightly with No. 4-0 sandpaper, and apply a second coat if necessary.

9. The deck, cabin, and spars of your boat may be finished to the natural color of the wood with clear transparent lacquer.

10. Apply one or two coats of thin white shellac to your deck, cabin, or spars. Sand lightly between coats with No. 4-0 sandpaper.

11. Apply or flow on two coats of clear lacquer. Sand very lightly with No. 4-0 sandpaper between coats.

12. The entire surfaces of your model boat may be given a final finish by rubbing with rottenstone and oil.

IV. FINISHING WITH STAIN AND VARNISH

Stain is used in finishing to give the wood the desired color, and to bring out the natural beauty of the grain. Oil-stains usually give better results than other stains. They may be purchased ready for use in any color or quantity, or they may be prepared by mixing colors in linseed-oil or turpentine.

1. Finish the hull of your boat first, by preparing the surfaces carefully.

2. Check all outside surfaces of your hull to be stained, and see that all tool-marks, chipped grain, and surplus glue, are entirely removed.

3. Sand the boat first with No. 0 sandpaper, and then with No. 4-0 sandpaper.

APPLYING THE STAIN

1. A dark mahogany stain or dark oak stain produces a good color on pine or basswood. You can stain the lower part of your boat with dark oak stain, and the section above the water-line with dark mahogany stain.

2. A small reed split in two makes a good water-line, especially if your boat is to be stained two colors. This reed is attached to the boat with glue and a few small brads. See Fig 27, Model A, the 38" Motor-Boat, page 55, and paragraph 9,

page 38, for further explanation on locating the water-line. Finish the reed before it is attached to the boat a dark green or dark blue.

3. Try out the stain to be used on the lower section of the boat on a piece of scrap wood, pine or basswood.

4. If the stain is too dark, add a little turpentine.

5. Procede to stain the lower section of the hull. Use a 1" brush, and brush with grain of the wood.

6. Remove the surplus stain by wiping with a clean cotton rag to produce an even shade. Follow the directions on the container.

7. In like manner, stain the upper part of the hull, using a red mahogany or a color of your choice.

8. Let the stain dry for at least twelve hours before proceeding with the finish.

APPLYING THE FILLER

1. If your hull is made out of an open-grain wood, it is best to fill the pores of the wood.

2. The use of paste wood-filler is the cheapest and quickest way of producing a smooth surface. A ½ lb. can of filler the color of your stain will do.

3. Do not sand the stained surface until after it has been filled.

4. Prepare the paste wood-filler by adding a small amount of turpentine to the filler. Stir the filler until you have a rather thin solution.

5. When you are satisfied the filler is of the right shade and thickness, cover the surface well with a brush.

6. Allow the filler to dry about 20 minutes, and wipe across the grain with coarse cloth, such as burlap. Wiping across the grain reduces the chances of removing the filler from the pores of the wood.

7. Check the surface of your hull to see that the wood is filled perfectly smooth.

8. Allow the filler to dry at least 24 hours, and then sand lightly with the grain, with No. 4-0 sandpaper.

9. We are now ready for a varnish finish.

APPLYING SPAR-VARNISH

Refer to the directions for applying spar-varnish, as given on page 38.

CHAPTER VI

THE "SILVER STREAK"—AN 18" MOTOR-BOAT

SOME BOYS are interested in model sailing yachts alone, while a great many boys are more interested in making a boat that runs by mechanical power, such as a model motor-boat. The "Silver Streak" is a small motor-boat that runs nicely in shallow and quiet water. It is especialy adapted to the smaller lakes or the playground wading pool.

Boys, you can build this fine motor-boat in your school shop; or probably you would rather make it at home in your own shop, during your leisure time. Many boys delight in building this model in my 7A and 8B classes. Take a look at Fig. 23, and watch the expression on these boys' faces as they are launching their "Silver Streak" motor-boats. They are settling a friendly argument of long standing, which originated in the school shop as to which one of the boats would make 50 yards in the least number of minutes.

The "Silver Streak"

Materials Required

(A) Hull, 1 pc, 2¾" x 4¼" x 18", pine
(B) Deck, 1 pc, ⅜" x 4¼" x 18", butternut or red gum
(C) Keel, 1 pc, ⅝" x 1" x 9¼", pine
(D) Rudder, 1 pc, 1" x 2", black iron, 20-gage
(E) Rudder-port, 1 pc, ³⁄₁₆" diameter x 2", brass tubing
(F) Rudder-rod and tiller, 1 pc, copper wire, 12-gage
(G) Rudder-guide, 1 pc, ¼" x ⁵⁄₁₆" x 2", red gum

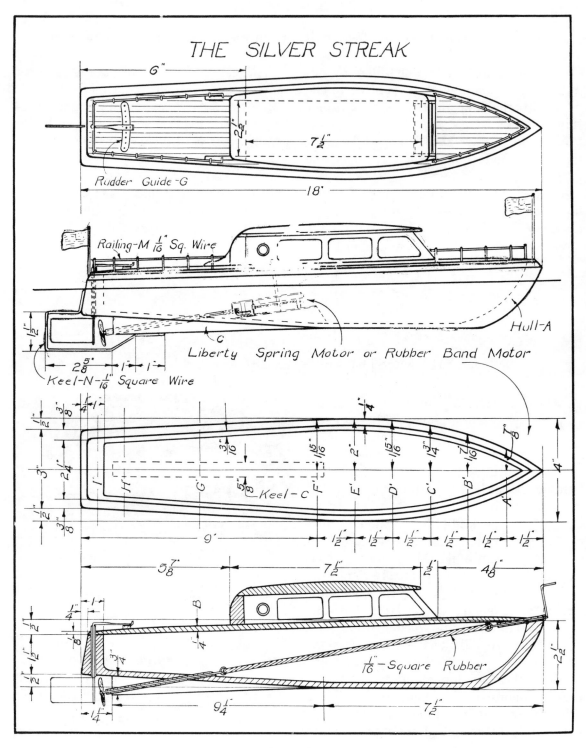

THE SILVER STREAK

PLATE IX

42

SILVER STREAK DETAILS

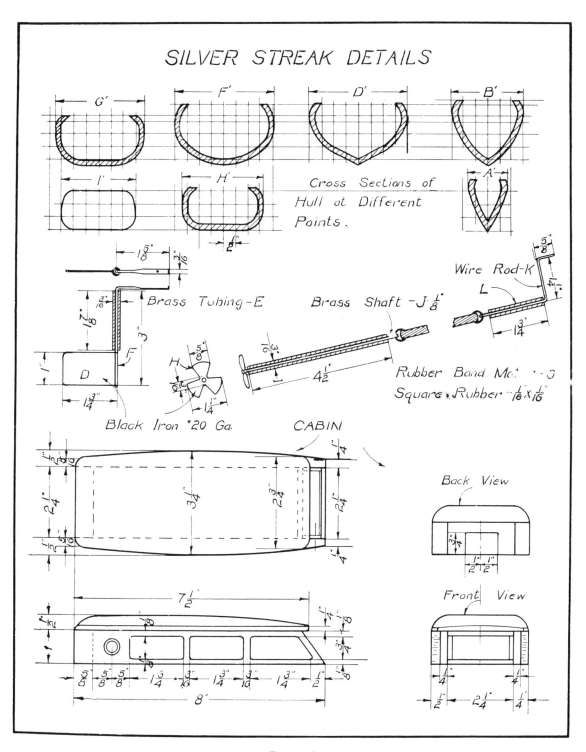

Cross Sections of Hull at Different Points.

Brass Tubing-E

Brass Shaft - J

Wire Rod-K

Rubber Band Mot...o
Square Rubber - $\frac{1}{16} \times \frac{1}{16}$

Black Iron #20 Ga.

CABIN

Back View

Front View

PLATE X

43

FIG. 23. Launching two "Silver Streaks" for a friendly test run

(*H*) Propeller, 1 pc, 2" x 2", black iron, 20-gage

(*I*) Propeller-shaft bearing, 1 pc, ¼" diameter x 4½" brass tubing

(*J*) Propeller-shaft, 1 pc, ⅛" diameter x 6", brass rod

(*K*) Handle, 1 pc, ⅛" diameter x 4", brass rod

(*L*) Handle-bearing, 1 pc, 3⁄16" diameter x 2", brass tubing

(*M*) Railing, 1 pc, 1⁄16" x 1⁄16" square, radio-wire

(*N*) Rudder-guard, 1 pc, same

Rubber motor, 4 yds., 1⁄16" x 1⁄16 square, rubber band

Liberty or spring motor, No. 309

Cabin

Sides, 2 pcs, ½" x 1⅛" x 8", red gum or butternut

Back, 1 pc, ⅝" x 1½" x 2¼", same

Top, 1 pc, ½" x 3½" x 8", same

Stand

Ends, 2 pcs, ⅜" x 1¾" x 4", same

2 pcs, ¼" diameter x 11¾", dowel-rod

Procedure

The Hull

1. Take a piece of white pine, 2¾" x 4¼" x 18½", and square it to the finished dimensions, 2½" x 4" x 18".

2. Lay out the hull, *A*, according to the drawing, Plate IX, and Fig. 24.

3. Use a pair of dividers and rule in spacing and measuring on each division line, A, B, C, etc.

4. Saw the corners with a cross-cut saw, as shown in Fig. 3.

5. With a spoke-shave, shape the sides of your boat, as shown in Fig. 4.

6. With a jack-plane, plane the top to

the deck-line, which slopes gradually from the bow to the stern of the boat. See Fig. 24.

7. In like manner the under back slope of the hull is planed.

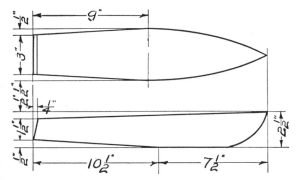

FIG. 24. Details of the hull of the "Silver Streak"

8. Nail a block to the top of the hull, as illustrated in Fig. 5 and Fig. 6. The hull can be held securely in the vise by this block while shaping the outside. The shaping of the outer part of the hull is the most important part of your boat. Do not rush your work at this point, but take plenty of time. Use a spoke-shave when shaping the outer part of the hull. See Fig. 6.

9. Check your hull often with the cross-section drawings, Plate X.

10. After the under part of the hull is shaped, make a 1/4" chamfer on the top edges of your boat, from the bow to about the center of the boat. From the center of the boat to the back, the edges are gradually rounded to the shape illustrated in Plate IX.

11. Make a cradle to hold the hull, while carving the inside part of the boat. The corners sawed from the round hull block, fastened to a rough board, can be used for the cradle. See Fig. 7. The hull can be held in a vice quite satisfactorily without

the cradle, but a device of this kind helps to make the work easier.

12. With a 3/4" gouge and a mallet, gouge out the inside of the hull until the walls are about 3/16" in thickness, except at the stern and bow.

13. Sandpaper the inside part of the hull with fine sandpaper. Make it as smooth as possible.

The Keel

14. Next, make the wedged-shaped keel, C, from a piece of pine, 5/8" x 1" x 9 1/4".

15. Fasten the keel to the hull with glue and small brads. The keel should be fastened at the center of the hull, 1 1/4" from the stern of the boat.

16. Bore a 3/16" hole in the keel, C, and in the bottom of the hull, A, to receive the propeller-shaft tube bearing, I. See detail drawing, Plate IX, for the angle of the shaft.

17. Give the inside part of the hull one or two coats of varnish.

18. Make a stand to support the hull. For details, refer to Fig. 25.

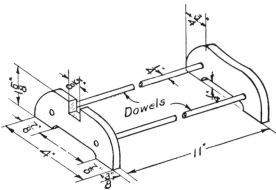

FIG. 25. Details of the stand for the "Silver Streak"

Propeller and Rubber Motor

1. Make the propeller, H, from black iron, 20-gage. Follow the detail drawing, Plate X, in making your propeller.

2. Drill a ⅛″ hole at the center of the propeller, and solder to the ⅛″ x 5″ brass rod, propeller-shaft, *J.*

3. Make the propeller-shaft bearing, *I,* from a piece of 3/16″ brass tubing. The brass tubing should be 4½″ long.

4. Insert a bushing, 1/16″ in thickness, between the propeller and tube bearing, *I.* The bushing may be cut from the 3/16″ brass tubing.

5. Insert the propeller-shaft, *J,* in the tube bearing, *I,* and flatten the top end of the shaft in a vise or with a hammer.

6. Bore a 1/16″ hole through this flat end of the shaft to receive the S-hook, for the square rubber motor.

7. The tube bearing, *I,* with propeller-shaft, can next be inserted in the 3/16″ hole in the keel and boat. Cement the tube in place with ship cement or ambroid.

8. Cut the handle bearing, *L,* from 3/16″ brass tubing.

9. Make the handle, *K,* from ⅛″ wire rod. Flatten one end of the ⅛″ wire, and drill a 1/16″ hole through this flat part, to receive the S-hook for the rubber motor.

10. Bore a 3/16″ hole through the front part of the hull to receive the tube-bearing, *L.* Insert, and cement bearing, *L,* in place.

11. Insert the wire rod, *K,* or crank-shaft in bearing, *L,* and bend the wire to handle shape. See detail drawing, Plate X.

12. Next, the square rubber motor can be attached to the shaft and crank-shaft, *K.*

Spring Motors

1. Three types of spring motor are described in Chapter IX. I have used the Liberty type probably more than any other.

2. If the Liberty spring motor is used, the propeller, propeller-shaft, and bearing, complete, are furnished with each motor.

Deck and Cabin

1. The deck for the "Silver Streak" can be made from either red gum or butternut. Shape the deck from a piece of wood, 5/16″ x 4″ x 18″, to correspond with the shape of the top of the hull.

2. Give the under part of the deck, *B,* a coat of varnish, and fasten the deck to the hull with glue and ½″ brads. Place the brads about 1¼″ apart. Set the heads of the brads below the surface of the wood.

3. The deck should have a curved top, from ¼″ at the center, rounded to ⅛″ to the sides and ends. This can best be done by planing the top part of the deck with a block-plane or a smooth-plane while the boat is held in a vise.

4. Cut out the hatchway next, 2½″ x 7″ and 6½″, from the back of the deck with a keyhole-saw. Or, the hatchway may be cut out before the deck is nailed to the boat, with a coping-saw, if preferred.

5. Make the cabin next. Square the side-pieces to the finished dimensions, ½″ x 1″ x 8″; the back-piece, to 5/8″ x 1″ x 2¼″; and the top to ½″ x 3¼″ x 7½″. Assemble the cabin with glue and small brads.

6. Shape the cabin according to the detail drawings, Plate X, after it has been assembled. Use block-plane, smooth-plane, and spoke-shave to plane and shape the cabin.

7. After the cabin is of the desired shape and size, cut out the window with a coping-saw. Bore a ¼″ hole in one corner of each window to insert the blade of the coping-saw.

8. Add a few more brads and set the heads below the surface of the wood. Sand the cabin with fine sandpaper.

Rudder and Rudder-Guide

1. Make the rudder, *D,* from a piece of black iron, 26-gage, 1″ x 2″.

2. Turn one edge with the wiring-machine or a pair of pliers, and solder to a piece of ⅛″ x 4¾″ brass rod, *F.*

3. Cut the rudder-port, *E,* from a piece of 3/16″ brass tubing.

4. Bore a 3/16″ hole through the hull, ¼″ from the stern, at a center point.

5. Insert and cement the rudder-port, *E,* in the 3/16″ hole.

6. Insert the brass rod, *F,* part of the rudder in the port, *E,* and bend the rod, *F,* to form the tiller, as shown in the detail drawing, Plate X.

7. Flatten one end of the tiller or arm until it is about 3/16″ wide. Bore a 1/16″ hole in the flat part of the tiller, ⅜″ from the end.

8. Make the rudder-guide, *G,* from a piece of hard wood.

9. Bore 1/16″ holes, ¼″ apart, to receive the pin that holds the tiller and the rudder in the position desired.

Finishing

1. The deck and the cabin are finished to the natural color of the wood. See Chapter V, "Methods of Finishing Model Boats."

Railing and Rudder-Guard

1. The railing, *M,* is made from 1/16″ square radio-wire, or copper wire, 16-gage.

2. Make the rail-posts 1¼″ long. File one end to a nail point, and make a loop on the other end to receive the wire rail.

3. Drive the posts into the deck, ¼″ from the edges of the deck, and 1½″ apart. Bore a small hole in the deck before driving each rail-post. Insert the rail wire through the loops in the posts.

4. Make the rudder-guard, or wire keel, *N,* from 1/16″ square wire, and flatten both ends of the wire with a hammer. Drill two 1/16″ holes in each of the two flat ends of the guard.

5. Fasten the guard to the back of the boat and the keel with ⅜″ brass screws.

Questions

1. What is the rudder used for?
2. Does a motor-boat need a keel?
3. Is lacquer water-proof?
4. What is the stern of your boat?
5. Why should the walls of your boat be as thin as possible?

Chapter VII

A 32″ SPEED-BOAT

HERE, BOYS, is that speedy motor-boat you have been looking for. It skims over the water like your Dad's mighty speed-boat. Just think of the fun of making a real motor-boat model, and the pleasure of sending that boat across your near-by lake at full speed. This speed-boat runs beautifully on two dry-cells, but better yet on three dry-cells.

Take a good look at the drawings and photographs of the 32″ speed-boat, and see if this is the model you would like to make.

You can construct this boat in your school shop; or, if you prefer, you can build it at home in your own work-shop.

Motor-boats of this type are always very

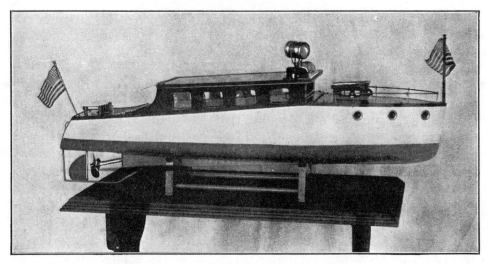

A 32″ Speed-Boat

popular with my 8A and 9B boys here at the Bryant Junior High School.

Materials Required

(A) Hull, 1 pc, 4⅜″ x 7¼″ x 33″, pine or bass
(B) Deck, 1 pc, 5⁄16″ x 7¼″ x 21½″, red gum, mahogany, or walnut
(C) Deck, 1 pc, ½″ x 7¼″ x 10½″, same
(D) Keel, 1 pc, ¾″ x 1¹⁄₁₂″ x 19¼″, pine
(E) Rudder, 1 pc, 2″ x 2½″, black iron, 20-gage
(C′) Rudder-shaft, 1 pc, ³⁄16″ diameter x 5¾″, brass rod
(F) Rudder-port, 1 pc, ¼″ diameter x 3¼″, brass tubing
(G) Tiller, 1 pc, ¼″ x 2½″, brass, 22-gage
(H) Rudder-guide, 1 pc, ¾″ x 4″, brass, 22-gage
(I) Propeller, 1 pc, 2″ x 2″, brass, 20-gage
(J) Propeller-shaft bearing, 1 pc, ¼″ diameter x 8½″, brass rod
(K) Propeller-shaft, 1 pc, ³⁄16″ diameter x 14″, brass rod
(L) Spot-light, front and rear parts of a flashlight
(M) Front lights, 2 flash-light batteries and bulbs
      Battery, 2 or 3 dry-cells
      Electric motor, see Chapter IX, "Motors"
(N) Railing, 1⁄16″ x 1⁄16″ square, radio-wire, or copper wire, 16-gage

Cabin

Sides, 2 pcs, ¼″ x 1⅝″ x 12¾″, red gum or mahogany
Back, 1 pc, ¼″ x 1¼″ x 4″, red gum, mahogany, or walnut
Top, 1 pc, ⅜″ x 6⅛″ x 12¾″, same

Stand

Front end, 1 pc, ½″ x 1¾″ x 6½″, red gum or walnut
Back end, 1 pc, ½″ x 2¾″ x 6½″, same
2 pcs, ½″ diameter x 12″, dowel-rod

Procedure

The Hull

1. Select a good solid block of pine or bass, plane it to the finished dimensions, 4¼″ x 7″ x 32″, and make the hull, A.

2. I find it rather hard to obtain solid pieces for model boats that are not checked, so I suggest that you build your hull from stock 1″ or 2″ in thickness. Make sure that you use a good grade of water-proof glue when gluing the hull. Leave the glued-up hull in clamps for at least 24 hours.

3. Lay out the hull, *A*, according to the 32″ speed-boat details, Plate XII. A center-line is drawn down the length of the hull, and ten lines A, B, C, etc., are drawn at right angles with the center-line.

4. Use a pair of dividers and rule in spacing and laying out the points on each division-line. Connect these points with a smooth-flowing curved line.

5. Saw the corners with a turning-saw or the band-saw; or, a crosscut-saw may be used. See Fig. 3.

6. With jack-plane and spoke-shave, shape the sides of your boat, as shown in Fig. 4.

7. The top of the hull slopes from a point 10½″ from the bow of the boat to the stern. Saw this surplus stock with the rip-saw, and plane to the deck-line with a jack-plane.

8. In like manner, the sloping under part of the boat can be cut and planed. See detail drawing, Plate XII.

9. Nail a block to the top of the hull, as illustrated in Fig. 5 and Fig. 6. By means of this block, the hull is held securely in the vise while shaping the outside.

10. Use draw-knife, jack-plane, and spoke-shave when shaping the bottom of the hull.

11. Make a cardboard or sheet-metal template for each of the half cross-sections, as shown in detail drawings, Plate XII. These templates will help in working the outside of the boat to the proper shape.

12. Check your hull often with these templates. When careful observation tells you that the shape is right, sand the hull carefully with fine sandpaper.

13. Shape the top edges of the hull by first making a ¼″ chamfer from the bow point of the boat down 10½″ on top of the hull. From this section to the back of the boat, the edges are gradually rounded with a spoke-shave.

14. Make a cradle to hold the hull, while gouging the inside. The corners sawed from the original block, fastened to a rough base-board, can be used for the cradle. See Fig. 7 and Fig. 14. The hull can be held in a vise quite satisfactorily without the cradle, but a device of this type helps to make the inside gouging easier.

15. Gouge out the inside of the hull next with a 1″ gouge and a mallet. Make the walls ¼″ in thickness, except at the bow and stern. In gouging the interior of the hull, the gouge and mallet should be handled very carefully.

16. Sandpaper the inside of the hull with No. ½ and fine sandpaper. Make the inside of your boat as smooth as possible. Do not leave it in a rough condition.

The Keel

1. Make the keel, *D*, from a piece of pine, ¾″ x 1¼″ x 19½″, formed to a wedge shape.

2. Fasten the keel, *D*, to the hull with glue and brads. The keel should be fastened to the center of the hull, and 5¾″ from the stern.

3. Bore a ¼″ hole in the keel, *D*, and into the bottom of the boat, to receive the propeller-shaft tube bearing, *J*. See the detail drawing, Plate XII, for the proper angle to bore the hole.

4. Give the inside part of the finished hull two coats of paint or varnish.

Decks

1. The main deck, *B*, and the front deck, *C*, can be made from red gum, mahogany, or walnut.

2. Shape the front deck, *C*, from a piece

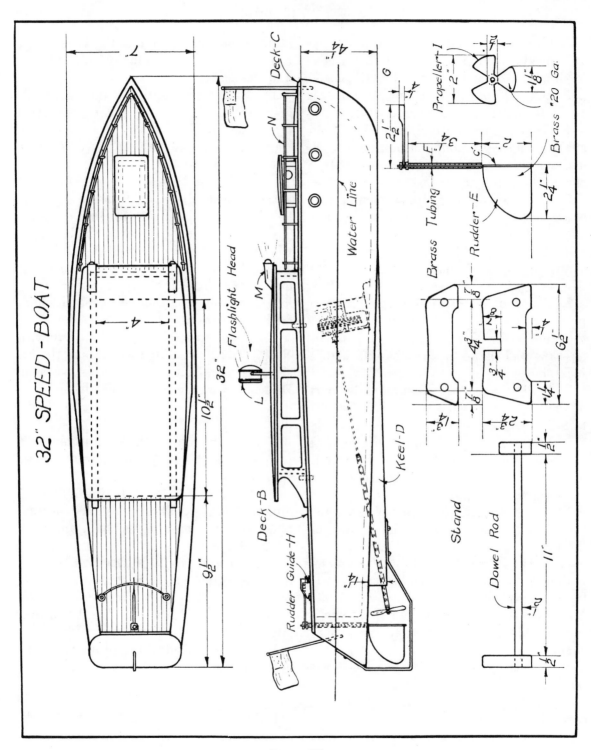

32" SPEED-BOAT

PLATE XI

50

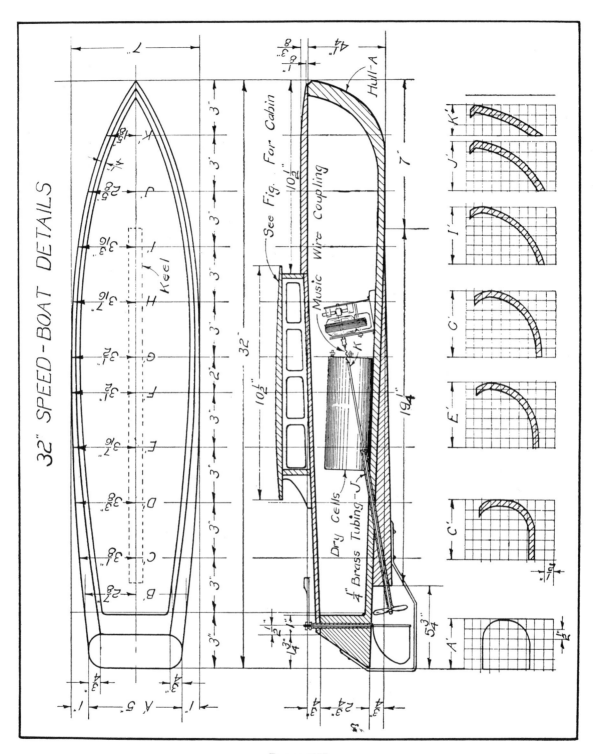

PLATE XII

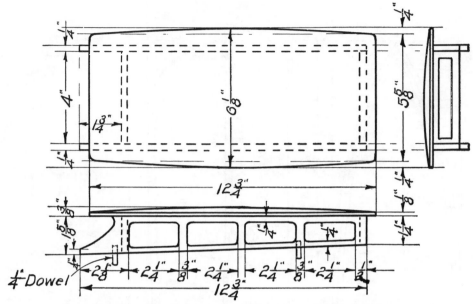

FIG. 26　Details of the cabin for the 32″ Speed-Boat

of wood, $\frac{3}{8}$″ x 7″ x $10\frac{1}{2}$″, according to the shape of the top of the boat.

3. This deck should have a curved top, from $\frac{3}{8}$″ at the center, rounded to $\frac{1}{8}$″ to the sides. The shaping of the top of the deck can best be done by tacking the deck, C, with a few brads, to a rough piece of board the shape of the deck. The deck is then held in the vise by this rough piece of wood while shaping the top of the deck with a block-plane or smooth-plane.

4. After the deck has been sanded smooth with fine sandpaper, make the lines, representing planking, with a knife and a straight edge. Make the lines about $\frac{1}{4}$″ apart, and about $\frac{1}{32}$″ deep. If you are careful with this job, the deck can be made to look very much like the real planked deck.

5. Make the deck, B, $\frac{1}{4}$″ in thickness. The planking lines on this deck may be cut before the deck is shaped, if you prefer.

6. Shape the deck, B, to fit the top of the

hull. Cut the opening for the cabin, 4″ x $10\frac{1}{2}$″ and $9\frac{1}{2}$″, from the back of the deck.

Cabin

1. Make the cabin according to the details shown in Fig. 26. Make the sides $\frac{1}{4}$″ thick, x $1\frac{5}{8}$″ high at the back, and $1\frac{1}{4}$″ high at the front, and $12\frac{3}{4}$″ long.

2. Cut out the windows with a coping-saw. Bore a $\frac{1}{4}$″ hole in one corner of each window to insert the blade of the coping-saw.

3. Make the front end, $\frac{1}{4}$″ x $1\frac{1}{4}$″ x 4″; and the back end, $\frac{1}{4}$″ x $1\frac{5}{8}$″ x 4″.

4. Make the top of the cabin $\frac{3}{8}$″ in thickness at the center, rounded to $\frac{1}{8}$″ to the sides.

5. Assemble the cabin with glue and $\frac{5}{8}$″ brads. Sand all parts to a smooth finish with fine sandpaper.

6. The cabin is attached to the deck by means of $\frac{3}{16}$″ dowels; two dowels being inserted in each side, Fig. 26. The cabin

can thus be easily attached to or detached from the deck at any time.

7. The deck and the cabin are finished in the natural color of the wood. See Chapter V, "Methods of Finishing Model Boats."

Propeller, Tube-Bearing, and Shaft

1. Make the propeller, *I*, from sheet-brass, 20-gage. Follow the detail drawing, Plate XI. Drill a ³⁄₁₆″ hole at the center of the propeller to receive one end of the shaft.

2. Cast propellers can be obtained already made in different sizes on the market.

3. Make the shaft, *K*, from a brass rod, ³⁄₁₆″ in diameter x 17½″ in length.

4. Solder the propeller to one end of the shaft. Drill a ¹⁄₁₆″ hole through the other end to receive the music-wire coupling.

5. Make the shaft-tube bearing, *J*, from ¼″ brass tubing, 8¼″ in length.

6. Insert a brass bushing ⅛″ in thickness between the propeller and the tube-bearing, *J*. Insert another bushing ⅛″ in thickness on the other end of the tube. Solder this bushing to the shaft so it will revolve with the shaft.

7. Before the propeller-shaft, *K*, is inserted in the tube-bearing, *J*, put some vaseline on the shaft. The vaseline will prevent the water from entering around the shaft, and it will cause the shaft to rotate freely.

8. The brass-tubing bearing can then be cemented or ambroided in the keel and boat in the proper place.

9. This part of your power-plant is very important, so be accurate in making the propeller, and in placing the bushings on the shaft.

Electric Motor

1. There are a number of small motors that work very well in this model boat. See Chapter IX, "Motors for Model Motor-Boats."

2. Make a wedge-shaped base of pine for your motor, and place the motor as accurately in line with the shaft as possible.

3. Use a piece of music-wire, .020, for the coupling or differential. Make the coupling the shape of a spring, winding the wire around a small round stick. Insert one end of the spring coupling through the hole in the shaft of the motor, and the other end through the hole in the propeller-shaft.

4. A paper-clip of appropriate size may also be used as a coupling, to connect the propeller-shaft to the motor.

5. The two or three dry-cells can be placed in the boat next. Place one dry-cell on each side of the propeller-shaft well towards the stern. A third cell can be added toward the front part of the boat. The dry-cells should be held in place by means of wooden cleats nailed to the bottom of the boat.

6. Wire the dry-cells to the motor and to a switch. The switch may be placed on top of the deck or in the cabin.

Fastening the Decks

1. After you are certain that your motor and dry-cells are installed in the right places, fasten the decks to your boat with glue and brads. You may attach the decks with ⅜″ round-head brass screws, if you prefer.

2. I suggest, however, that the decks be fastened permanently to the boat with glue, and brads; for there is plenty of room, by removing the cabin, to get at the motor, or to replace dry-cells.

Rudder and Guide

1. Make the rudder, *E*, from sheet-brass, 20-gage, 2″ x 2½″. Make it of the shape shown in detail drawing, Plate XI.

2. Turn one edge of the rudder with the wiring-machine or a pair of pliers, and solder to a piece of brass rod, ³⁄₁₆″ x 6″.

3. The brass rod, *C'*, can be split on one end with a hack-saw, to receive the rudder, instead of turning one edge, if preferred. Solder the rod to the rudder.

4. Thread the top end of rudder-rod, *C*.

5. Cut the rudder-port, *F*, from a piece of brass tubing, ¼″ diameter x 3½″ in length.

6. Bore a ¼″ hole through the back of the deck and hull, ⅜″ from the stern, at a center point. Insert and cement the tube-port, *F*, in the ¼″ hole.

Tiller

1. Make the tiller, *G*, from sheet-brass, 20-gage, ¼″ wide and 2½″ in length. Twist one end of the tiller, as shown in the drawing.

2. Insert the brass rod part of the rudder in the port, *F*. Lock the tiller to the rudder-rod, *C'*, with two brass nuts.

Rudder-Guide

1. Make the rudder-guide, *H*, from a piece of sheet-brass, 24-gage. Drill a ⅛″ hole in each end of the metal, and then make it of the shape shown in the drawing, Plate XI. Cut slits in the top edge of the guide, to receive the tiller. These openings should be about ³⁄₁₆″ apart.

2. Attach the guide to the deck, *B*, with ⅜″ x 4 brass screws.

Rudder-Guard and Railing

1. The railing can be made from ¹⁄₁₆″ x ¹⁄₁₆″ square radio-wire, or copper wire, 16-gage. Solder the rail-posts to the railing at points about 1½″ apart. Sharpen each rail-post to a nail-point.

2. Drill small holes in the deck before driving the rail-posts into the deck.

3. Make the guard for rudder and propeller from ⅛″ x ⅛″ square radio-wire, and flatten each end of the wire with a hammer. Drill two ¹⁄₁₆″ holes in each end of the guard, about ⅜″ apart.

4. Fasten the guard to the stern and the keel with ⅜″ x 4 round-head brass screws.

Boat-Stand

1. Your speed-boat is not complete unless you have a stand for it when it is not in use.

2. A suggested boat-stand is given in detail drawing, Plate XI.

3. The ends of the stand can be made from red gum, or the same kind of wood as that used on the decks of the boat.

4. The ends of the stand are connected with hardwood dowels, as shown.

Finishing

1. See Chapter V, "Methods of Finishing Model Boats."

Questions

1. What is meant by the term, *buoyancy*?

2. What is meant by the center of gravity in model boat building?

3. Has the paint finish of your boat any effect on the speed of the boat?

4. Why use bushings on your propeller-shaft?

Chapter VIII

A 38″ MOTOR-BOAT

Model A

HERE, BOYS, you can have the thrilling satisfaction of owning a handsome motor-boat, that slips smoothly through the water, with the speed of a mighty cruiser. See Fig. 27. This is the Prize-Winning 38″ Motor-Boat that was published in the *Industrial Education Magazine* some time ago,[1] with certain added refinements and improvements which have resulted from our experiments with that model.

So many boys throughout the country have written to me for detailed plans of this boat, that I have decided to include it in this book. Many of these cruisers are built each semester in my 9th-grade classes.

[1] See, "A 38-Inch Motor-Boat Model," by the author; *Industrial Education Magazine*, Vol. XXX, No. 6, December, 1928, pages 223-225. Awarded First Prize, Annual I-E-M Competitions, 1928, Class B, Shop Problems in Woodworking.

Materials Required

(A) Hull, 1 pc, 5⅝″ x 8½″ x 38″, pine or bass
(B) Deck, 1 pc, 5/16″ x 8½″ x 22″, mahogany or walnut
(C) Deck, 1 pc, ½″ x 8½″ x 17″, same
(D) Keel, 1 pc, ¾″ x 1⅜″ x 20″, pine
(E) Rudder, 1 pc, 1¾″ x 3½″, brass, 20 gage
(F) Rudder-port, 1 pc, ¼″ diameter x 4″, brass tubing
(G) Tiller, 1 pc, ¼″ x 3″, brass, 22-gage
(H) Rudder-shaft, 1 pc, 3/16″ diameter x 3½″, brass rod
(I) Rudder-guide, 1 pc, ¾″ x 5″, brass, 22-gage
(J) Propeller, 1 pc, 2¼″ x 2¼″, brass, 20-gage
(K) Propeller-guard, 1 pc, ⅛″ x ⅛″ square x 12″, radio-wire
(L) Propeller-shaft bearing, 1 pc, ¼″ diameter x 11″, brass tubing
(M) Propeller-shaft, 1 pc, 3/16″ diameter x 15″, brass rod

Fig. 27. The 38″ Motor-Boat, Model A

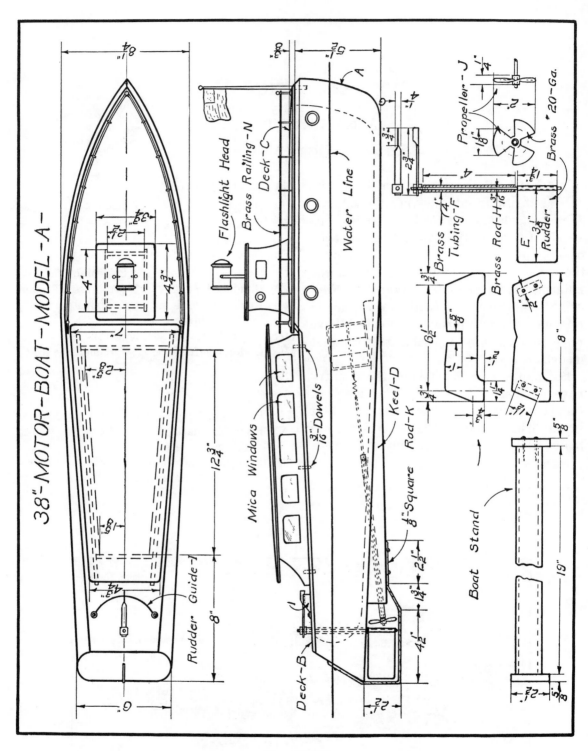

PLATE XIII

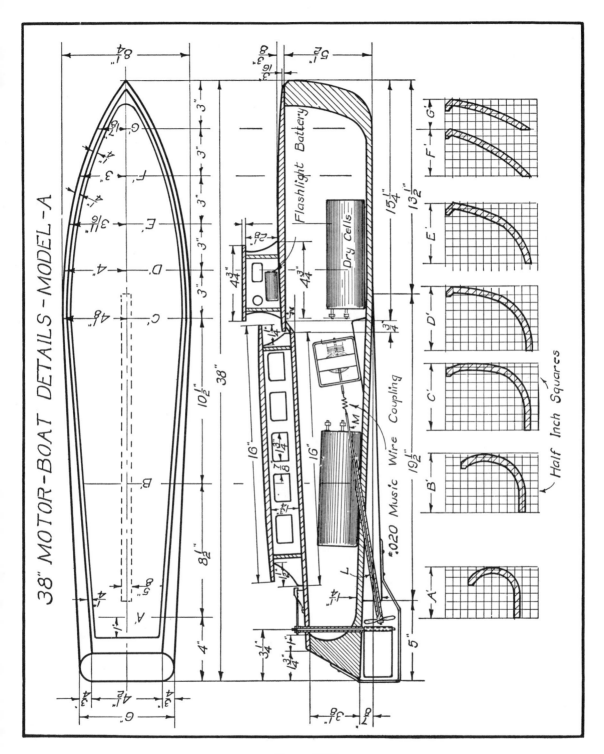

38" MOTOR-BOAT DETAILS — MODEL — A

PLATE XIV

57

(N) Railing, $\frac{1}{16}''$ x $\frac{1}{16}''$ square, radio-wire
Electric motor, See Chapter IX, Motors
Battery, 4 dry-cells
Spot-light, front and rear parts of a flash-
    light
Spot-light battery, 2 flash-light batteries

Cabin

Sides, 2 pcs, $\frac{1}{4}''$ x $1\frac{3}{4}''$ x 16'', mahogany
    or walnut
Front, 1 pc, $\frac{1}{4}''$ x $1\frac{3}{4}''$ x $5\frac{1}{4}''$, same
Back, 1 pc, $\frac{1}{4}''$ x $1\frac{3}{4}''$ x $3\frac{1}{4}''$, same
Top, 1 pc, $\frac{3}{8}''$ x 7'' x 16'', same

Pilot-House

Sides, 2 pcs, $\frac{3}{16}''$ x 2'' x $4\frac{1}{2}''$, same
Front and back, 2 pcs, $\frac{3}{16}''$ x 2'' x $2\frac{1}{2}''$,
    same
Top, 1 pc, $\frac{1}{4}''$ x $3\frac{3}{4}''$ x $4\frac{3}{4}''$, same

Stand

Ends, 2 pcs, $\frac{5}{8}''$ x $2\frac{1}{2}''$ x 8'', same
Sides, 2 pcs, $\frac{1}{2}''$ x $1\frac{1}{2}''$ x 19'', same

Procedure

The Hull

1. The making of the 38'' motor-boat may be organized on a semiproduction plan. This is, a part of the work, such as getting out stock, gluing up the hulls, and making the rudders, can be accomplished under production methods. While the designing, gouging of the hull, construction of cabins, metal parts, the wiring, adjustment of parts, assembling, and finishing can be made individual jobs.

2. If, however, a boy chooses to make a cruiser model at home, he will do all the work himself.

3. Build your hull, *A*, from stock 1'' or 2'' in thickness. Select a good grade of water-proof glue when gluing the hull. Leave the glued up hull in clamps for at least 24 hours.

4. Lay out the hull, *A*, according to the detail drawing, Plate XIV. A center-line is drawn down the length of the hull, and seven lines, A, B, C, etc., are drawn at right angles with the center-line.

5. On each line, A, B, C, measure and lay out points according to the dimensions given in the drawing. Connect these points to form a smooth curve for the sides of the boat.

6. Saw the corners with a turning-saw or the band-saw.

7. With jack-plane and spoke-shave, shape the sides of your boat, as shown in Fig. 4.

8. The top of the hull slopes from a point 16'' from the bow to the stern. Saw off this surplus stock with a rip-saw, and plane to the deck-line with a jack-plane. Study the cross-section, Plate XIV, for details.

9. The bottom of the stern of the boat is completed in a similar manner.

10. Nail a block to the top of the hull, as illustrated in Fig. 5 and Fig. 6. The hull is securely held in the vise while shaping the outside.

11. Use draw-knife, jack-plane, and spoke-shave when shaping the bottom of your boat. See Fig. 6.

12. Make a cardboard or sheet-metal template for each of the half-sections, as shown in the cross-section drawing, Plate XIV.

13. Check your hull often with these templates. This device will help in getting the outside of the boat to the desired shape.

14. When you are satisfied that your hull is the correct shape, sand it carefully with fine sandpaper.

15. Round off the top of the back section of your boat according to the detail drawing, Plate XIV.

16. Make a cradle to hold the hull, while

gouging the inside of the boat. The corners sawed from the original block, fastened to a rough base-board, can be used for the cradle. See Fig. 7 and Fig. 14.

17. The hull can be held in a vise quite satisfactorily without the cradle, but a device of this type helps to make the inside gouging easier.

18. Gouge the inside of the hull next, with a 1¼" gouge and mallet. Make the walls ¼" in thickness, except at the bow and the stern of the boat. In gouging the interior of the hull, the gouge and mallet should be handled very carefully.

19. Sandpaper the inside of the hull with No. ½ and fine sandpaper. Make the inside as smooth as possible. Do not leave it in a rough condition.

Keel

20. Make the keel, D, from a piece of pine ⅝" x 1¼" x 19½", to a wedge shape.

21. Fasten the keel, D, to the hull with glue and brads. The keel should be fastened to the center of the hull. and 5" from the stern.

22. Bore a ¼" hole in the keel, D, and into the bottom of the hull, to receive the propeller-shaft tube bearing, L. See the detail drawing, Plate XIV, for the proper angle to bore the hole.

23. Give the inside of the finished hull two coats of paint or varnish.

Decks

1. The deck, B, and the front deck, C, can be made from mahogany, walnut, or red gum.

2. Shape the front deck, C, from a piece of wood, ⅜" x 8½" x 17", according to the shape of the top of the front part of your boat.

3. The deck, C, should have a curved top, from ⅜" at the center, rounded to ⅛" to the sides.

4. The shaping of the top of the deck can best be done by tacking it with a few brads to a rough piece of board the shape of the deck. The deck is then held in the vise by this rough piece of wood while shaping the top with a block-plane or smooth-plane.

5. After the deck has been sanded smooth with fine sandpaper, make the lines representing planking, with knife and straight-edge. Make the lines about ¼" apart, and little better than 1/32" deep. If you are careful with this job, the deck can be made to look very much like the real planked deck.

6. Make the deck, B, ¼" in thickness. The planking lines on this deck may be cut before the deck is shaped, if you prefer.

7. Shape the deck, B, to fit the shape of the aft part of the hull. Cut the opening for the cabin, 4¾" wide at the back, 7" wide at the front, and 12¾" long. The rear of the opening should be 6¼" from the rear of the deck, B.

Cabin and Pilot-House

1. Make the cabin according to the drawings, Plate XIV. Make the sides, ¼" x 1¾" x 16", and cut out the windows with a coping-saw. Bore a ¼" hole in one corner of each window to insert the blade of the coping-saw before sawing.

2. Make the front end, ¼" x 1¾" x 7"; and the back end, ¼" x 1¾" x 4¾".

3. Make the top of your cabin 5/16" in thickness at the center, rounded to ⅛" to the sides.

4. Assemble the cabin with glue and ⅝" brads. Sand all parts of your cabin to a smooth finish with fine sandpaper.

5. The cabin is attached to the deck by means of ³⁄₁₆″ dowels. The cabin can thus be easily attached to or detached from the deck of your boat at any time.

6. The decks, cabin, and pilot-house are finished to the natural color of the wood. See Chapter V, "Methods of Finishing Model Boats."

7. See detail drawing for pilot-house, Plate XIV.

Propeller, Tube-Bearing, and Shaft

1. Make the propeller, *J*, from sheet-brass, No. 20-gage. Follow the details in the drawing, Plate XIII. Drill a ¼″ hole at the center of the propeller to receive a ¼″ bushing. Insert and solder this ¼″ bushing as a part of your propeller.

2. Cast propellers for model boats may be purchased in different sizes, in the rough, or finished ready for use.

3. Make the shaft, *M*, from a brass rod, ³⁄₁₆″ in diameter and 13½″ in length.

4. Solder the propeller to one end of the shaft. Drill a ¹⁄₁₆″ hole through the other end of the shaft to receive the music-wire coupling.

5. Make the shaft-bearing, *L*, from ¼″ brass tubing, 11½″ in length.

6. Insert a brass bushing, ⅛″ in thickness, between the propeller and the tube bearing, *L*. Insert another bushing, ⅛″ in thickness, on the other end of the tube, *M*. Solder this bushing to the shaft so it will revolve with the shaft.

7. Before the propeller-shaft is inserted in the tube-bearing, *L*, put some vaseline on the shaft. The vaseline will prevent the water from entering around the shaft, and it will cause the shaft to rotate freely.

8. The brass tube-bearing can then be cemented or ambroided in the keel and boat in the proper place.

Electric Motor

1. There are a number of small motors that work very well in this model boat. See Chapter IX, "Motors for Model Motor-Boats."

2. Make a pine base for the motor, wedge-shaped.

3. Place the motor as accurately in line with the shaft as possible. Attach the motor to the base with ⅜″ round-head screws.

4. Use a piece of music-wire, No. 020, for the coupling or differential. Make the coupling the shape of a coil spring by winding the wire around a small stick. Insert one end of the spring coupling through the hole in the shaft of the motor, and the other end through the hole in the propeller-shaft. See Fig. 28. A small paper-clip also serves as an excellent coupling.

5. The four dry-cells may be placed in the boat next. Place one dry-cell on each side of the propeller-shaft, well towards the stern of the boat. Place the other two dry-cells as near the center of the boat as possible. The dry-cells should be held in place by means of wooden cleats nailed to the bottom of the boat.

6. Wire the dry-cells to the motor. Allow for lead-in wires to a switch, to be placed on the deck, *B*, or in the cabin.

Fastening the Decks

1. After you are certain that your motor and dry-cells are installed in the right places, fasten the decks to your boat with glue and brads.

2. You can attach the decks with ¾″ round-head brass screws, if you prefer. I suggest, however, that the decks be fastened permanently to the hull with glue

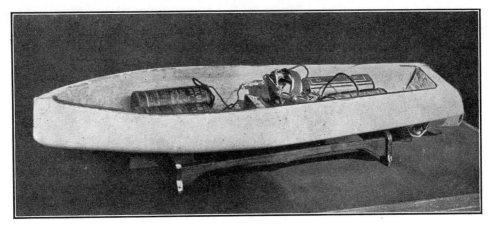

FIG. 28. Installing the power-plant in the 38″ Motor-Boat

and brads, for there is plenty of room by removing the cabin to get at the motor, or to replace dry-cells.

Rudder and Guide

1. Make the rudder, E, from sheet-brass, No. 20-gage, 1¾″ x 3½″, as shown in the drawing, Plate XIII.

2. Turn one edge of the rudder with the wire-machine or a pair of pliers, and solder to a piece of brass rod, ³⁄₁₆″ x 6½″.

3. The rudder-rod, H, can be split on one end with a hack-saw, to receive the rudder, instead of turning one edge, if preferred. Solder the rod to the rudder, as in the first method.

4. Thread the top end of the rudder-rod, H.

5. Cut the rudder-port, F, from a piece of ¼″ brass tubing, ¼″ in diameter x 4″ in length.

6. Bore a ¼″ hole through the deck and the hull, 1½″ from the back of the deck, at a center point.

7. Insert and cement the tube-port, F, in the ¼″ hole.

8. Make the tiller, G, from sheet-brass, No. 22-gage, ¼″ wide and 2½″ long. Twist one end of the tiller, as shown in the drawing, Plate XIII.

9. Insert the brass-rod part of the rudder in the port, F. Lock the tiller to the rudder-rod, H, with two brass nuts.

10. Make the rudder-guide, I, from a piece of sheet-brass, No. 22-gage. Drill a ⅛″ hole in each end of the metal, and then make it the shape shown in the drawing, Plate XIII. Cut openings on the top part of your guide to receive the tiller. The openings should be about ³⁄₁₆″ apart.

11. Attach the guide, I, to the deck, B, with ⅜″ No. 4 brass screws.

Propeller-Guard and Railing

1. The railing can be made from radio-wire, ¹⁄₁₆″ x ¹⁄₁₆″ square, or copper wire, No. 16. Solder the posts to the railing, about 1½″ apart. Sharpen each post to a nail-point.

2. Drill small holes in the deck before driving the posts into the deck.

3. Make the propeller-guard from radio-wire, ⅛″ x ⅛″ square, and flatten each end of the wire with a hammer.

4. Drill two ¹⁄₁₆″ holes at each end of the guard wire, about ⅜″ apart.

5. Fasten the guard to the stern of the boat and the keel with 3/8″ No. 4 round-head brass screws.

Boat-Stand

1. It is necessary to have a boat-stand to place your boat on, when it is not on the water. A suggested stand is shown in the detail drawing, Plate XIII.

2. The stand may be made from wood that matches the deck and cabin. The stand is assembled with 1½″ No. 8 round-head screws and finished to the natural color of the wood.

Finishing

1. See Chapter V, "Methods of Finishing Model Boats."

Questions

1. Why is a good paint job necessary?
2. What is meant by the cock-pit or hatchway?
3. Why should the inside of the boat be painted?

38″ MOTOR-BOAT—MODEL B

IN THE 38″ Motor-Boat, Model B, we have a motor-boat of cruiser speed-boat type. See Fig. 29. With the exception of the deck-line, the deck, the sedan cabin, the back cabin, and the speedier motor, this model is built on the same lines and dimensions as Model *A*, Fig. 27.

Materials Required

With the exception of the following items, use the same list of materials as that specified for the 38″ Motor Boat, Model A, page 55:

Hull

(*A*) Hull, 1 pc, 4¾″ x 8½″ x 38″, pine or bass
(*B*) Deck, 1 pc, 3/8″ x 8½″ x 38″, red gum or mahogany

Sedan Cabin

Sides, 2 pcs, ¾″ x 1½″ x 12″, same
Back, 1 pc, ¾″ x 1½″ x 4½″, same
Top, 1 pc, 5/8″ x 6″ x 11½″, same

Back Cabin

Sides, 2 pcs, ¼″ x 1″ x 8″, same
Top, 1 pc, ¼″ x 4″ x 4¾″, same
Motor, 1 automobile-horn motor

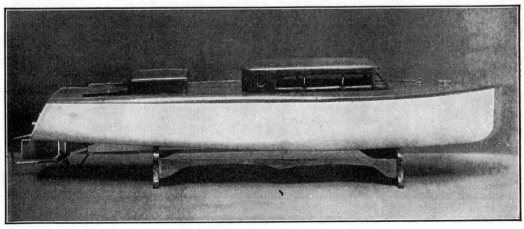

FIG. 29. The 38″ Motor-Boat, Model B

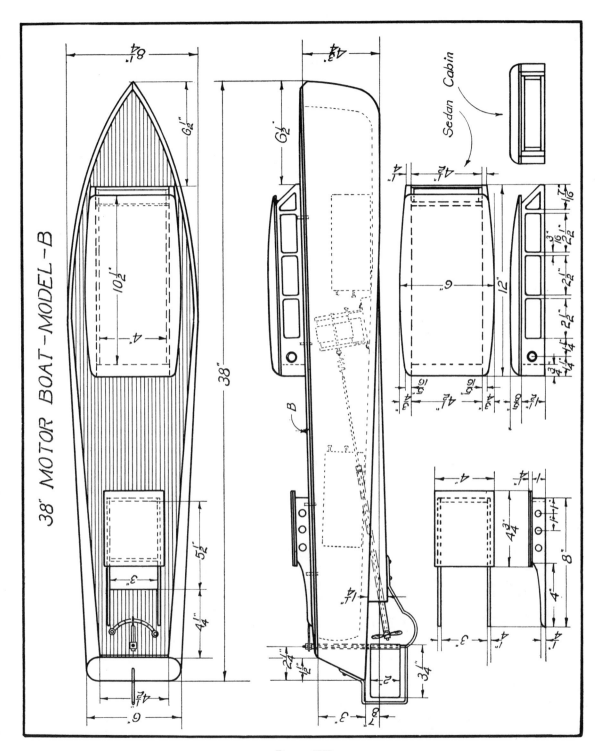

PLATE XV

63

Procedure

1. Follow the directions given for building Model A, in the construction of Model B, with the exception of the top part of the hull, the deck, and the sedan and back cabins.

2. Note in the drawing, Plate XV, that the hull is 4¾″ in thickness at the bow, and 3″ at the stern.

Deck

1. The deck for this Model B motor-boat may be made from red gum or mahogany, either of which will finish up very nicely in the natural color of the wood.

2. Shape the deck from a piece of wood, ⅜″ x 8¼″ x 38″, to fit the top of the hull.

3. The shaping of the top can best be done by tacking the deck, B, with a few brads, to a rough board the shape of the deck. The deck can be held in the vise by the rough board, while shaping the top with a block-plane or smooth-plane.

4. The deck should have a curved top, from ⅜″ at the center rounded to ⅛″ to the sides.

5. After the deck has been sanded smooth with fine sandpaper, make the planking lines with knife and straight edge. Make the lines about ¼″ apart and 1/32″ deep.

6. Cut the opening for the cabins next. Cut the opening for the sedan cabin 4″ x 10½″, and 6½″ from the bow of the boat. The back opening should be 3″ x 5½″, and 4½″ from the stern.

Cabins

1. Make the sedan cabin according to the detail drawing, Plate XV. Make the sides ¾″ x 1½″ x 12″; the back, ¾″ x 1½″ x 4½″; and the top, ⅝″ x 6″ x 11½″; use red gum or mahogany.

2. Assemble the cabin with glue and 1½″ brads. Set the heads of the brads below the surface of the wood.

3. Shape the sides and the top of your cabin after it has been assembled, by using a block-plane or smooth-plane.

4. After the cabin is of the desired shape and size, cut out the openings for the windows with a coping-saw.

5. The detail drawings, Plate XV, show clearly how the back cabin is made.

6. The two cabins are attached to the deck by means of 3/16″ dowels; thus they may easily be attached or detached at any time.

7. Give the under part of your deck two coats of varnish or white lead, before fastening the deck to the boat.

Fastening the Deck

1. After you are certain that the motor and dry-cells are installed in their proper places, fasten the deck to the boat with glue and 1″ brads. Or you may attach the deck with ½″ No. 4 round-head brass screws, if you prefer. I suggest, however, that the deck be fastened permanently to the hull with glue and brads; for there is enough room, by removing the cabins, to get at the motor or to replace dry-cells.

2. Fill all nail-holes in the deck and the cabins with a filler the color of the wood. Fine sandpaper dust sanded from your deck or cabins, mixed with glue, will produce a good filler.

3. The deck and cabins should be finished to the natural color of the wood. See Chapter V,″ Method of Finishing Model Boats.″

CHAPTER IX

MOTORS FOR MODEL MOTOR-BOATS

THE boy builder of model boats sometimes has difficulty in locating a suitable motor for his motor-boat. I have received many inquiries concerning the types of motor that can be used on model motor-boats of different sizes. Following is a description of some of the motors that have proven very successful in the boats constructed by my boys here in Minneapolis.

Rubber-Band Motor

Probably the simplest method of propelling a model boat is by means of rubber bands. To be driven successfully by rubber bands, the boats should be of the smaller type, not over 10″ to 20″ in length. Boys derive a great deal of pleasure and enjoyment from small boats driven by rubber-band motors.

The rubber motor used on the model motor-boat is similar to that used by the model airplane builder. See Fig. 30, No. 1.

The rubber motor designed for the "Silver Streak," Chapter VI, is installed inside the boat, and gives very satisfactory results; however, a rubber motor will also work very efficiently in the water. In this case, the motor is attached beneath the hull of the boat.

The rubber motor is wound up with a model-airplane winder, or a winder con-

FIG. 30. Spring-motors and rubber-band motor suitable for the "Silver Streak"

FIG. 31. Electric motors and spring-motors suitable for 32″ and 38″ Motor-Boats

structed out of an egg-beater. Or, as in the case of the "Silver Streak," the motor may be wound up with a crank. See Chapter VI, Plate X.

Spring Motors

The spring motor shown in Fig. 30, No. 2, is a very satisfactory type for small boats, such as the "Silver Streak." It is quite speedy, and will drive such a boat for a distance of 200 feet or more. It is necessary, however, to line up the propeller-shaft with the motor-shaft very accurately.

Several types of motor, of which this is one, may be purchased from manufacturers of and dealers in mechanical toys and amateur construction supplies and devices. In some cases, the complete assembly may be purchased, including: motor, propeller, propeller-shaft, and bearing-tube.

The spring motor shown in Fig. 30, No. 3, is taken from an inexpensive toy truck. This type of motor gives a very good account of itself when installed in a model boat. The propeller, propeller-shaft and tube may be constructed according to the directions given for the "Silver Streak," Chapter VI.

There are a number of toys and small vehicles to be found in the stores, from which the motors may be detached, to be used in model boats with very satisfactory results. A trip of inspection through the toy and novelty stores, with this particular purpose in mind, is an interesting experience for any boy.

The motor taken from a toy phonograph, for example, shown in Fig. 30, No. 4, makes a fairly satisfactory motor for a small boat. The phonograph motor is a low-speed motor; consequently, it is necessary to make some changes and adjustments, in order to bring the speed transmitted to the propeller up to a point that is suitable for driving the boat.

Electric Motors

I do not believe there can be any question that the most satisfactory method of propelling model boats is some type of electric motor. In this case, the boat must be large enough to accommodate the motor, and at least two dry-cells. The motor-boats illustrated in this book are all large enough to accommodate from two to four dry-cells.

The ideal means for driving the motor is a storage-battery, if you have the necessary time and skill, and are willing to go to the trouble of making one.

The problems of selecting an electric motor, or of learning where to obtain such a motor, seems to be a common stumbling-block for the boy who is building a model motor-boat. I have received many inquiries on this subject from boys who have been interested in the Prize-Winning 38-Inch Motor-Boat, described in Chapter VIII.

As in the case of the spring motors, there are a number of types of electric motor, suitable for driving the propeller of a model boat, which may be found in the stores specializing in toys and electric novelties. One of the best of these is illustrated in Fig. 31, No. 1. This is a powerful little motor, and works very well in the 32″ and 38″ boats, operating on two or three dry-cells. It is necessary to drill a hole in the shaft of the motor, 1/16″ in diameter, to receive the spring coupling.

Another type of motor is found in the mechanical construction sets, consisting of metal parts and devices, of which the toy and novelty stores display several varieties. One of these motors is shown in Fig. 31, No. 2. It is light and efficient, and operates well on two dry-cells. However, it works more efficiently on three or four dry-cells. A model motor-boat driven by one of these motors will do from five to seven miles per hour.

Drill a hole in the shaft of the motor, near the end, $\frac{1}{16}''$ in diameter, to receive the wire coupling. In order to secure the best results, be sure that the shaft of the motor and the shaft of the propeller are accurately in line.

The junior electric motor, shown in Fig. 31, No. 3, is a motor that is constructed as a class project in the electric shop at Bryant Junior High School, Minneapolis. Many motors of this type are constructed in the school shop each term. This is a six-volt motor, and performs very efficiently on three or four dry-cells.

The motor in an automobile horn makes a speedy and very satisfactory power-plant for the model motor-boat. Did you ever think of looking in "Uncle Joe's" automobile graveyard for a motor? Most cars today are equipped with six-volt storage-batteries; therefore, the usual horn functions on six volts or less. The motor

from almost any automobile horn of the six-volt type will do for your boat, and will operate very nicely on three or four dry-cells.

Two such motors are shown in Fig. 31, No. 4 and No. 5, and are very satisfactory for the 32'' and 38'' boats. In order to reduce the weight somewhat, parts of the frame are cut away, as shown in No. 4.

A discarded horn may be purchased at any salvage yard at small expense, and in many cases all that is needed is proper cleaning and lubrication, adjustment, and possibly a new set of brushes.

The motor from a medium-sized phonograph, shown in Fig. 31, No. 6, is very satisfactory, especially for a model of the cruiser type. Such a motor has a strong spring, and a long voyage can be obtained. Since it is a low-speed motor, some changes and adjustments are necessary, to build up the required speed.

If you have difficulty in finding a suitable spring motor or electric motor in your local stores, write a letter to the publisher of this book, THE MANUAL ARTS PRESS, 237 North Monroe Street, Peoria, Illinois; and you will be given instructions as to where they may be secured.

CHAPTER X

THE ANNUAL MODEL-BOAT REGATTA

THE Annual Model-Boat Regatta of the Bryant Junior High School, Minneapolis, is always a delightful and exciting event for the boys; and not only for those who have entries in the various

contests, but for hundreds of onlookers as well. For the benefit of readers who may wish to work up a Regatta, I offer the set of Rules and Regulations which we have found very satisfactory, as follows:

RULES AND REGULATIONS

I. Time and Place

At 2:30 p.m., Friday, June 7.
At Powderhorn Park Lake.

II. Prizes

1. A silver cup will be awarded by the Bryant Junior High School Model Boat Club to the first-place winner in each Class.

2. A silver cup will be awarded to the best constructed Model Sailing-Yacht and to the best constructed Motor-Boat.

III. Who May Compete

1. Any boy who has constructed a model boat in the manual-arts shops at Bryant Junior High School may compete in the contests.

2. A competitor must be attending Bryant Junior High School at the time of the contests.

3. A boy who has made a boat at home in his own shop may compete in the contests.

Note.—More than 150 model boats have been entered in a single contest at Bryant Junior High School Regattas.

IV. Classes of Events

1. Construction:
   (a) The best constructed model sailing-yacht.
   (b) The best constructed model motor-boat.
2. Model Sailing-Yacht Races:
   (a) Yachts under 21″.
   (b) Yachts from 21″ to 35″.
   (c) Yachts 36″ and over.
3. Model Motor-Boat Races:
   (a) Boats under 21″, rubber motor.
   (b) Boats under 21″, spring motor.
   (c) Speed-Boats from 21″ to 35″, electric motor.

(d) Cruiser-type boats, 36″ and over, electric motor.

V. Suggestions

1. Join the Bryant Junior High School Model Boat Club.

2. Encourage your boy friends to build model boats at home, if they cannot possibly make them in the School shops.

3. Make sure that you have a good paint job on your boat.

4. Do not wait until the day of the contests to experiment with the sails on your model yacht.

5. Make sure that the motor in your motor-boat is in perfect condition before you put the boat in the water.

6. Have the batteries fully charged before the start of the race.

VI. Officials

Note.—The manual-arts instructors of Bryant Junior High School are always more than glad to act as Judges, and to assist in other ways, in order to make the Regatta a success.

MINNEAPOLIS PARK BOARD
CONTESTS FOR SAILING-YACHTS AND
MOTOR-BOATS

For the past several years the Recreation Department of the Minneapolis Park Board has conducted an Annual Contest for Model Sailing-Yachts and Model Motor-Boats, usually during the early part of August. The following set of Rules and Regulations is typical.

RULES AND REGULATIONS

I. Time and Place

Preliminary district meets are scheduled for Saturday, August 10th, at 2:30 p. m., in all city parks in which there is a suitable body of water. *Note.*—In Minneapolis seven lakes, each of approximately one square mile area, four lagoons of one-fourth square mile each, and eleven small park pools are now available for these meets.

The Final meet will be held at Loring Park Lake, Saturday, August 17th, at 2:30 p. m.

II. Prizes

Gold, silver, and bronze medals will be awarded to first, second, and third place winners, respectively, in the Preliminary meets.

Silver cups will be awarded to first, second, and third place winners in the Final meet.

III. Who May Compete

Any boy or girl under 16 years of age, residing in Minneapolis, may compete.

IV. Events

1. Construction:
   (a) The best constructed sailing-yacht
   (b) The best constructed motor-boat

2. Speed:
   Model Sailing-Yachts
   (a) Under 21".
   (b) From 21" to 35".
   (c) 36" and over.

   Model Motor-Boats
   (d) Under 21".
   (e) From 21" to 35".
   (f) 36" and over.

V. Point Awards

Points will be awarded in each event as follows:
First place, 5.
Second place, 3.
Third place, 1.

VI. Entries

A meeting of playground instructors will be held on Saturday, August 3d, at which time entries for the contests will be received; and daily thereafter, from Monday, August 5th, to Friday, August 9th.

VII. Additional Suggestions and Rules

1. No commercial or purchased boat will be admitted to the contests.

2. Organize a Playground Sailing and Motor Boat Club in your neighborhood, and be ready.

3. There are hundreds of boys in Minneapolis who own boats. All you need to do is to interest them in your contest.

4. Invite adult sailing and motor enthusiasts to assist you in developing your meet.

5. Immediately following each Preliminary Meet, the instructor in charge should mail in to the office a complete list of the first, second, and third place winners in each class.

6. Keep the bulletin-board on your playground full of information, suggestions, and ideas on the building of boats, and on the coming contests.

7. Some of the things to advertise are:
   Time and place of contests.
   Prizes to be awarded.
   Lists of entries.
   Pictures of sailing-yachts and motor-boats.
   Newspaper articles.
   Lists of names of boosters.

8. Notify the director promptly if any unusual feature develops that can be used in newspaper publicity.

PART II

MODEL AIRPLANES

CHAPTER XI

THE "MIDGET FLYER"

HERE IT IS, Boys, that "Midget Flyer," that will do 100 seconds or more in the air indoors. It can take off on its own power like a real cabin plane or a tri-motor plane. If you are a beginning model-airplane enthusiast, try this model as your first flying plane. You are sure to get good results, and many hours of enjoyment, if you follow the directions carefully. Many hundred small planes of the "Midget Flyer" type are built each year at the Bryant Junior High Airplane Club, here in Minneapolis.

The "Midget Flyer"

Materials Required

(A) Fuselage, 1 pc, $\frac{1}{16}$" x $\frac{5}{32}$" x $8\frac{1}{4}$", balsa

(B) Bearing, 1 pc, music-wire, or aluminum, .016

(C) Rear hook, 1 pc, same, $1\frac{1}{2}$" long

(D) Can, 1 pc, same, $1\frac{1}{2}$" long, .013 or .016

Wing

(E) Elevator, 1 cross-piece, $\frac{1}{64}$" x $\frac{1}{32}$" x $3\frac{3}{4}$", bamboo
    1 pc, 4" x 4", Japanese tissue-paper

(F) R u d d e r, 1 pc, frame, $\frac{1}{64}$" x $\frac{1}{32}$" x 6", bamboo
    1 pc, 2" x2", Japanese tissue-paper

(G) Leading edge, 1 pc, $\frac{1}{16}$" x $\frac{5}{32}$" x $11\frac{1}{4}$", balsa

(H) Trailing edge, 1 pc, $\frac{1}{16}$" x $\frac{5}{32}$" x 12", balsa

(I) Ribs, 3 pcs, $\frac{1}{64}$" x $\frac{1}{64}$" x $2\frac{1}{8}$", bamboo

(J) Clips, 2 pcs, music-wire, .016 x $2\frac{1}{2}$" long

(K) Covering, 1 pc, 3" x 14", Japanese tissue-paper

Power Plant

(L) Propeller, 1 pc, $\frac{7}{16}$" x $\frac{5}{8}$" x 5", balsa

(M) Propeller-shaft, 1 pc, music-wire, .016 x 3" long

(N) Washers, 1 or 2 small beads

(O) Motor, 1 pc, $\frac{1}{16}$" x $\frac{1}{16}$" square x 20", rubber band
    Ambroid, or household cement, small quantity

A group of young model airplane builders at Bryant Junior High School, Minneapolis

Procedure

1. Cut a piece of balsa, $\frac{3}{32}''$ x $\frac{3}{16}''$ x $8\frac{1}{4}''$, for the fuselage, and sand it to the finished dimensions, $\frac{1}{16}''$ x $\frac{5}{32}''$ x $8\frac{1}{4}''$, with No. 4-0 sandpaper. See A, Plate XVI.

2. Make sure that your motor-stick or fuselage, A, is not thicker or wider than the dimensions given. Remember, the lighter the plane, the longer the flight.

3. Cut a groove, $\frac{1}{32}''$ x $\frac{3}{16}''$, under the rear end of the fuselage to receive the rudder. Also cut a notch, $1''$ from the rear end, to receive the cross-piece.

4. Pine, bass, or butternut may be used instead of balsa, if balsa is not obtainable in your district. A "Midget Flyer" made from bass wood or butternut will make 10 to 18 seconds in the air.

5. Balsa is the best and only wood to use in model-airplane construction if you are looking for the pleasure of seeing that plane of yours stay up minutes instead of seconds.

Bearing

1. Make the front bearing, B, from a piece of No. .016 music-wire, or a piece of No. 26-gage aluminum. A small brad flattened with a hammer can also be used.

2. If you choose the aluminum or brad, drill a hole through the metal with a No. 70 drill or phonograph-needle, and bend the bearing to an L-shape, as shown in the drawing, Plate XVI.

3. The wire bearing made from No. .016 music-wire is probably the easiest to make. Make a small loop on one end of the wire, by bending the wire around a fine brad or a needle. Use small round-nose pliers for this job.

4. Ambroid or cement the bearing, B, to the top of the front end of your fuselage, A. A drop or two of ambroid will hold the bearing securely to the fuselage. Be sure that the ambroid or cement is dry before proceeding with this part of the plane.

Rear Hook

1. Bend the rear hook, C, from a piece of No. .016 music-wire, to the shape shown in the drawing, Plate XVI. Shape this wire hook with round-nose pliers, and cement it to the rear end and top of the fuselage.

2. The center part of the loop of the rear hook should be about $\frac{3}{16}''$ from the fuselage, and in line with the hole in the front bearing, B.

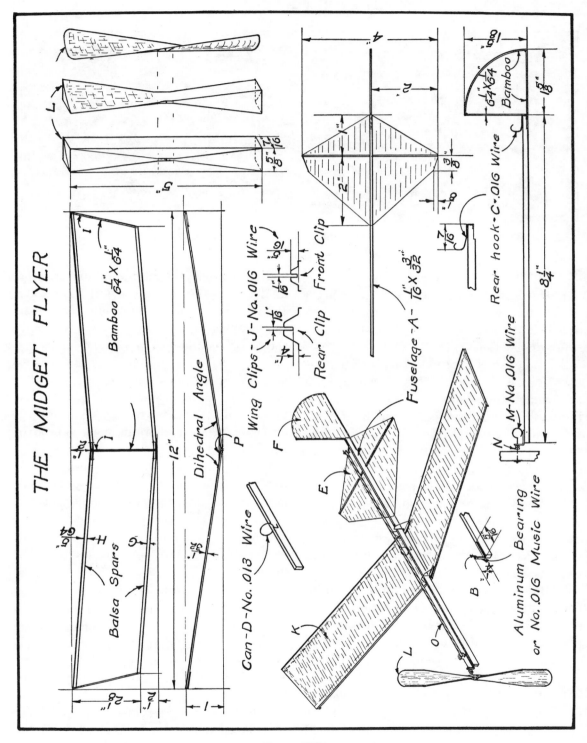

THE MIDGET FLYER

PLATE XVI

72

Can or Guide

1. Shape the can or guide, *D*, from No. .016 or No. .013 music-wire, and cement it to the center part of the fuselage.

2. The can should extend a little over ¼″ above the fuselage, just so it clears the rubber motor.

Rudder

1. Make the rudder-frame, *F*, from ¹⁄₆₄″ x ¹⁄₃₂″ bamboo next. Use the smooth part of the bamboo.

2. Draw the shape of the rudder-frame on a piece of wood, and insert a number of small brads on the outline.

3. Bend the bamboo piece by warming it over a flame and then bending around the form. Make sure that the bamboo is uniform in thickness and width.

4. Cement the vertical piece of the rudder to the bottom section of the rudder-frame.

5. Make sure that the bottom part of your rudder extends about ³⁄₁₆″ beyond the vertical piece.

6. The extended horizontal piece should be cemented to the fuselage next, fitting nicely in the small groove under the back part of the fuselage. A drop of ambroid will hold the rudder in place.

Elevator

1. Cut a strip of bamboo, ¹⁄₃₂″ x ¹⁄₃₂″ x 4″, for the cross-piece of the elevator.

2. Cement this cross-piece in the small notch made in the motor-stick, 1″ from the back.

3. Use Japanese tissue-paper to cover the elevator and the rudder It is well to make a pattern for the elevator from heavy paper such as a drawing paper first. Draw around the pattern on tissue-paper to lay out your elevator.

4. Some boys use a silk thread outline on the elevator. This makes the elevator stronger, but a bit heavier. If the Japanese tissue-paper is ironed out smooth, it works very nicely without the thread outline, and the plane will be lighter.

5. Paint the rudder-frame and the under part of the fuselage and the elevator cross-piece with a thick banana-oil, and attach the tissue-paper. Trim off surplus paper with a razor-blade when the paper is dried.

The Wing

1. Make the leading edge, *G*, of the wing, ¹⁄₁₆″ x ⁵⁄₆₄″ x 11¼″, and the trailing edge, or spar, *H*, ¹⁄₁₆″ x ⁵⁄₆₄″ x 12″, from balsa. Make sure that these spars are of the proper thickness and width.

2. Cut three ribs, ¹⁄₆₄″ x ¹⁄₆₄″ x 2⅛″, in size.

Wing-Form

1. This method of using a wing-form, to hold the spars in place and to insure the proper angle in the wing, is the best way of bending the wings I know of. The form can be used not only as a bending device, but also as a wing holder when the plane is not in use. Make the form according to Fig. 32 and Fig. 32A, from a piece of pine, 1″ x 2½″ x 13″.

2. The angle of the V-shaped block represents the dihedral angle that you will have in your wing. The purpose of the dihedral angle, or V-shaped wing, is to give the plane stability; or, in other words, to keep the plane steady while flying.

3. Draw the outline of the wing on the wing-form with a pencil.

4. Bend the two wing-spars, leading edge, *G*, and trailing edge, *H*, at the center of each spar. If the balsa is brittle. use hot water or steam in bending.

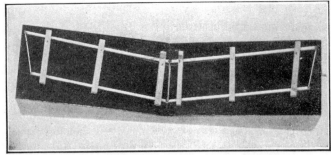

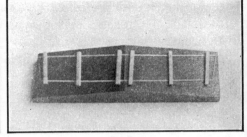

FIG. 32. Wing-form for the "Midget Flyer"   FIG. 32A

5. Place the bent spars in the wing-form, on the outline, and nail four or five wood cleats across the spars to hold them in place. When nailing the cleats, make sure that you barely touch the balsa spars.

6. Glue a small V-block of balsa at the center of each spar. These V-blocks, *P*, are very small and light, but they help to keep the wing the proper shape.

7. Cement the three ribs in their proper places, one in the center, and the others on the ends. A drop of ambroid on each end of each rib will hold the spars securely together.

Wing-Clips

1. Make the two wing-clips from No. .016 music-wire. Bend the clips according to the forms shown in the drawing, Plate XVI, with round-nose pliers. Be sure that the center opening of each clip is bent to fit the fuselage tightly.

2. The higher clip is the rear clip, and is $5/16''$ higher than the front clip. The difference in the heights of the two clips gives the wing an upward slant, to make the wing climb. This upward slant is called the *angle of incidence,* and should be checked very carefully.

3. When the clips are the proper shape, cement them exactly in the center of the wing-spars, on top of the V-blocks, *P*.

4. Take two pieces of Japanese tissue, $2\frac{1}{4}'' \times 7''$, and iron them out, so there will be no wrinkles. Cut the paper to fit around the clips.

5. Paint the top of the spars and ribs with thick banana-oil, and attach the paper, starting at the center rib and working out to the tip. It is best not to paint the whole wing at one time, but just a part at a time.

6. Work carefully when applying the banana-oil and attaching the paper, to insure smoothness of paper and a neat job.

7. When the wing is completely covered, trim the edges with a razor-blade.

Propeller

1. The success of making a real flying model depends to a great extent on the propeller. The propeller, by revolving at a high rate of speed, pulls the model craft through the air. The propeller is probably the hardest part of the plane to make, and should receive much careful and painstaking attention. I suggest that you experiment with pine or bass, before attempting to make your propeller of balsa.

2. Cut a block for the propeller, $7/16'' \times 5/8'' \times 5''$, from a good straight-grained piece of balsa. Sand it on all sides smoothly.

3. Mark out the blank by drawing lines from corner to corner diagonally. Make a small hole at the intersection of the lines,

at the exact center of the block, with a pin. See, *L,* Plate XVI.

4. Carve the propeller-block to these lines, leaving the center part of the block ⅛" thick or more. This part is left thicker, to prevent breaking while carving the blades.

5. Draw the end diagonal lines next. These diagonal lines show the end shape and pitch of your propeller, and should run in opposite directions on the two ends.

6. Carve out the blades of the propeller carefully, until they are ¹⁄₁₆" thick, and of the proper shape.

7. Finish the propeller with fine sandpaper, No. 4-0. When complete, the blades should not be over ¹⁄₃₂" in thickness, and at the hub not more than ¹⁄₁₆".

8. Sand the ends of your propeller round, with fine sandpaper.

Propeller-Shaft

1. Make the propeller-shaft, *M,* from No. .016 music-wire. See details, in Plate XVI.

2. Make a loop on one end of the shaft, and insert the shaft in the propeller, as shown.

3. Make a small U-bend in the wire, and ambroid the wire securely to the propeller.

4. Place one or two small beads on the shaft, to cut down the friction between the bearing and the propeller.

Motor

1. The power on this "Midget Flyer" is obtained from a piece of square rubber band, ¹⁄₁₆" x ¹⁄₁₆" x 18", or two strands of rubber tied in a square knot. There should be about a ¾" slack when the motor is attached to the fuselage.

Landing-Gear

1. Nearly every boy likes to have a landing-gear on his model airplane, especially a small type of plane.

2. A landing-gear for the "Midget Flyer" can be made from fine music-wire, No. .013, or from fine strips of bamboo.

Adjusting and Flying the "Midget-Flyer"

1. Attach the wing to the fuselage at a point close to the elevator.

2. After you have assembled your plane, allow the plane to glide from your hand, to test its balance and stability.

3. Wind the motor (propeller) about 25 to 50 times, and make necessary adjustments.

4. If the plane tries to climb too rapidly, set the wing back.

5. If it dives quickly, set the wing forward a little, and try the plane again.

6. When you are satisfied that your "Midget Flyer" glides evenly, wind the motor about 200 times for trial flights.

7. Since the "Midget Flyer" is an indoor plane, you will want the plane to fly in a circle, the size of the circle depending on the size of the room, auditorium, or hall. By curving the rudder to the left (on a right-handed propeller), the plane will be caused to follow a circular path.

8. The rudder can be bent by holding it close to the mouth and breathing on it, while bending it a little at a time with your fingers.

9. The rudder can be attached to the fuselage with a slight curve in it, when the plane is assembled.

Questions

1. What is meant by the leading edge and trailing edge?

2. What is the angle of incidence?

3. What is meant by the dihedral angle in an airplane

Chapter XII

THE "JUNIOR ENDURANCE FLYER"

The "Junior Endurance Flyer"

HAVE you ever watched a goose flying high above your head, with its long neck extended far in front of its body? Well, the "Junior Endurance Flyer" in the air resembles the flight of a goose, only you can control your plane and make it fly indoors in a large circular path as well as outdoors.

The "Junior Endurance Flyer" can do from five to ten minutes in the air when flying outdoors, and at least two minutes when flying indoors in a fairly good-sized auditorium. This airplane is not hard to make, and is one of the best flying models known. See Plate XVII.

Materials Required

(*A*) Fuselage, 1 pc, $\frac{5}{32}$" x $\frac{5}{16}$" x 16", balsa

(*B*) Bearing, 1 pc, music-wire, .020, or aluminum

(*C*) Rear hook, 1 pc, music-wire, .020 x $1\frac{1}{2}$" long

(*D*) Can, 1 pc, music-wire, .016 x $1\frac{1}{2}$" long
   S-hook, 1 pc, music-wire, .020 x $1\frac{1}{2}$" long

(*E*) Elevator, 1 cross-piece, $\frac{1}{32}$" x $\frac{1}{32}$" x $6\frac{1}{4}$", bamboo
   1 pc, $5\frac{1}{2}$" x $6\frac{1}{2}$", Japanese tissue-paper

(*F*) Rudder, 1 pc, lower, $\frac{1}{64}$" x $\frac{1}{32}$" x $4\frac{1}{8}$", bamboo
   1 pc, vertical, $\frac{1}{64}$" x $\frac{1}{32}$" x $3\frac{3}{4}$", bamboo
   1 pc, diagonal, $\frac{1}{64}$" x $\frac{1}{32}$" x $3\frac{1}{4}$", bamboo
   2 pcs, back section, $\frac{1}{64}$" x $\frac{1}{32}$" x 1", bamboo

Wing

(*G*) Leading edge, 1 pc, $\frac{1}{16}$" x $\frac{1}{8}$" x 20", balsa

(*H*) Trailing edge, 1 pc, $\frac{1}{16}$" x $\frac{1}{8}$" x 21", balsa

(*I*) Ribs, 3 pcs, $\frac{1}{32}$" x $\frac{1}{16}$" x $3\frac{1}{4}$", bamboo

(*J*) Tips, 2 pcs, $\frac{1}{32}$" x $\frac{1}{16}$" x $3\frac{3}{8}$", bamboo

(*K*) Corner-braces, 4 pcs, $\frac{1}{16}$" x $\frac{1}{4}$" x $\frac{5}{8}$", balsa

(*L*) Clips, 2 pcs, music-wire, .020

(*M*) Covering, 1 pc, $3\frac{1}{2}$" x 24", Japanese tissue-paper

Power-Plant

(*N*) Propeller, 1 pc, $\frac{5}{8}$" x $1\frac{1}{4}$" x 11", balsa

(*O*) Propeller-shaft, 1 pc, music-wire, .020 x 4" long

(*P*) Washers, 2 beads, medium size

(*Q*) Motor, 1 pc, $\frac{1}{8}$" x 34", flat rubber band

(*R*) Landing-skid, 1 pc, $\frac{1}{32}$" x $\frac{1}{32}$" x 12", bamboo

Procedure

Fuselage

1. For the fuselage, or motor-stick, *A,* cut a piece of balsa, $\frac{1}{4}$" x $\frac{3}{8}$" x 16", and sand it to the finished dimensions, $\frac{5}{32}$" x $\frac{5}{16}$" x 16", with No. 4-0 sandpaper. Make the motor-stick of uniform thickness and width the full length.

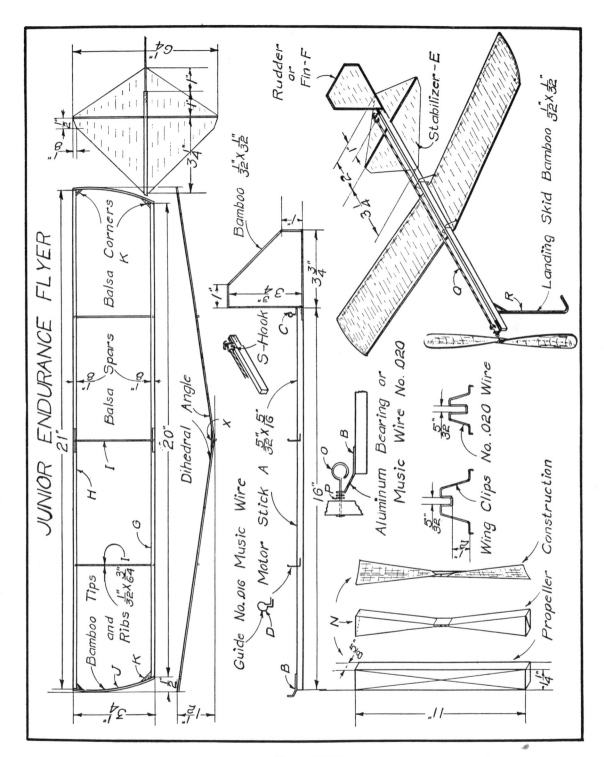

JUNIOR ENDURANCE FLYER

Rudder or Fin-F

Stabilizer-E

Landing Skid Bamboo $\frac{1}{32}$ X $\frac{1}{32}$

Balsa Corners K

Balsa Spars

Balsa

Dihedral Angle

Bamboo $\frac{1}{32}$ X $\frac{1}{32}$

Bamboo Tips and Ribs $\frac{1}{32}$ X $\frac{3}{64}$ I

S-Hook

Guide No..016 Music Wire

Motor Stick A $\frac{5}{32}$ X $\frac{5}{16}$

Aluminum Bearing or Music Wire No. 020

Wing Clips No..020 Wire

Propeller Construction

PLATE XVII

77

2. Cut a groove, $\frac{1}{32}''$ in thickness and $\frac{3}{8}''$ in length, under the rear end of the fuselage to receive the lower section of the rudder. Also, cut a small notch on the under part of the fuselage, 1" from the rear end, to receive the cross-piece of the elevator.

3. Balsa wood is the only wood to use on your model, if you are working for an endurance record with your plane.

Launching the "Junior Endurance Flyer"

Bearing

1. Make the front bearing, *B*, from a piece of No. .020 music-wire, a piece of No. 24-gage aluminum, or a brad flattened down with a hammer. If you choose the aluminum or the flat brad, drill a hole through the metal with a No. 70 drill, and bend the bearing to an L-shape, as shown in the drawing, Plate XVII. A phonograph-needle can be used for a drill quite successfully also.

2. Cement the bearing, *B*, to the top of the front end of the fuselage, *A*. A drop or two of ambroid will hold the bearing securely to the fuselage. Be sure that the ambroid or cement is dry before proceeding with the rest of the fuselage.

Rear Hook

1. Make the rear hook, *C*, from a piece of No. .020 music-wire, of the shape shown in the drawing, to fit the rear end of the fuselage. Use a small round-nose pliers to shape the eye or hook.

2. Insert and ambroid the rear hook in the end of the fuselage or motor-stick.

3. The center of the eye or the loop of the rear hook should be about $\frac{5}{16}''$ from the top of the fuselage, and in line with the hole in the front bearing.

Guide or Can

1. The guides or cans are to prevent the fuselage from bending and breaking when the rubber is wound up.

2. Make two cans from No. .016 music-wire. The top of the cans or guides should extend a little above the rubber.

Rudder

1. Make the rudder, *F*, from bamboo, $\frac{1}{64}''$ x $\frac{1}{32}''$. Use strips of bamboo with the shiny side.

2. Draw the shape of the rudder frame on a piece of wood, and insert a number of small brads on this outline. Build the rudder frame around these brads, and glue the pieces together with ambroid while they are flat on the pattern board. Make sure that the lower part of the rudder extends $\frac{3}{8}''$ beyond the vertical piece.

3. The extended horizontal piece should be cemented to the fuselage next, fitting nicely in the groove under the rear of the fuselage. A drop or two of ambroid or cement will hold the rudder securely in place.

4. If you wish to fly your plane indoors, curve the rudder a little to the left when cementing the rudder to the fuselage.

Elevator

1. Make the cross-piece of the elevator or stabilizer, *E*, from bamboo, $\frac{1}{32}''$ x $\frac{1}{32}''$ x $6\frac{1}{4}''$.

2. Cement this cross-piece in the small notch made in the motor-stick, 1" from the rear. The cross-piece should be at a right angle with the motor-stick.

3. Use Japanese tissue-paper to cover the elevator and the rudder.

4. It is well to make a pattern for the elevator from heavy paper, such as drawing-paper, before cutting the tissue-paper covering. Draw around the pattern on the tissue-paper, to get the proper size of elevator. The tissue-paper should be ironed out nice and smooth before being attached to the elevator and rudder.

5. Paint the rudder-frame and the under part of the motor-stick and elevator cross-piece with a thick banana-oil. Fasten your tissue paper quickly before the oil dries.

6. Trim off the surplus tissue paper with a razor blade when the paper and oil are dry.

The Wing

1. Make the leading edge of the wing, *G*, $\frac{1}{16}''$ x $\frac{1}{8}''$ x 20", and the trailing edge, *H*, $\frac{1}{16}''$ x $\frac{1}{8}''$ x 20", from balsa wood. Make sure that these edges (or spars) are of uniform thickness and width.

2. Cut the three ribs, *I*, $\frac{1}{32}''$ x $\frac{1}{16}''$ x $3\frac{1}{4}''$, and the two wing-tips, *J*, $\frac{1}{32}''$ x $\frac{1}{16}''$ x $3\frac{3}{8}''$, from bamboo.

Wing-Form

1. The wing-form is a very helpful device in holding the wing in place while bending the spars and assembling the different parts. The form can also be used as a holder when the plane is not in use to prevent the wing from warping. See Fig. 33 and Fig. 33A.

2. Make the form according to the dimensions shown in Fig. 34, from a piece of pine, 2" x 4" x 22"; or it may be constructed from heavy cardboard. The angle or V-shaped opening in the form represents the dihedral angle that you will have in your wing.

The purpose of the dihedral angle or V-shaped wing is to give the plane stability; or, in other words, to keep the plane steady while flying.

3. Draw the outside outline of the wing on the form with a pencil. Make sure that the tips are outlined also.

4. Apply hot water or steam to the center portions of the two spars, and bend them to the V-shape of the wing-form.

5. Place the bent spars in the wing-form, on the outline, and nail five or six wood cleats across the spars with small brads to hold them in place. See Fig. 33. When nailing the cleats, make sure that you

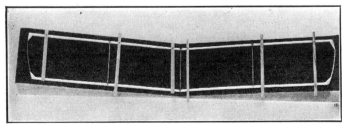

FIG. 33. Wing-form for the "Junior Endurance Flyer"

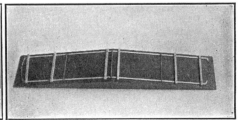

FIG. 33A

barely touch the balsa spars with the cleats.

6. Glue a V-block of balsa $\frac{1}{16}$" x $\frac{1}{8}$" x $\frac{5}{8}$", at the center of each spar. These V-blocks, X, help to keep the wing in the proper shape.

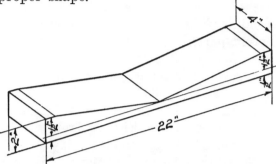

FIG. 34.   Details of the wing-form for the "Junior Endurance Flyer"

7. Cement the ribs in their places according to the drawing. Use small brads on the outline to hold the bent bamboo tips to the shape shown in the drawing.

8. The small balsa corners suggested in the drawing are really very helpful in making the wing strong and solid. Use ambroid in fastening these small reinforcement pieces to the wing.

Wing-Clips

1. Make the two wing-clips from No. .016 music-wire. Bend the clips according to the dimension given in the drawing, Plate XVII. Use round-nose pliers in bending the clips. Be sure that the center opening of each clip is bent to fit the fuselage or motor-stick tightly.

2. The higher clip is the rear clip, and is $\frac{1}{2}$" higher than the front clip. This difference in the heights of the two clips gives the wing an upward slant, to make the plane climb. This upward slant is known as the *angle of incidence,* and should be checked very carefully.

3. When you are satisfied that the clips are of the right size and shape, cement them exactly in the center of the wing spars, on top of the small V-blocks, X.

4. Take a piece of Japanese tissue-paper, 3" x 23", and iron it out, so that the paper will be smooth without wrinkles. Cut the paper to fit around the wing-clips.

5. Paint the top of the spars, ribs, and tips with the thick banana-oil. Paint only a part of the wing at a time, and attach the paper, starting at the center rib, and working out to the tips of the wing. Work carefully when applying the banana-oil and attaching the paper, to insure smoothness of paper and a neat job. A smooth surface of the wing is very essential to good flying.

6. When the wing is completely covered, and the oil and paper are thoroughly dried, trim the surplus paper with a razor-blade.

Propeller

1. Make the propeller for the "Junior Endurance Flyer," $\frac{5}{8}$" x $1\frac{1}{4}$" x 11", from balsa wood. The endurance record you expect to get out of your plane depends a great deal on the propeller. The propeller, therefore, should be carefully carved out and well balanced.

2. Mark the block from which the propeller is to be made, by drawing fine lines diagonally on one flat surface of the block. Make a small hole at the intersection of these lines, at the exact center of the block, with a pin or No. .020 music-wire.

3. Carve the block to the diagonal lines, leaving the center part of the block $\frac{1}{4}$" thick. This part is left thicker, to prevent breaking while carving the blades.

4. Draw the end diagonal lines, which show the end shape and the pitch of the propeller.

5. Carve out the blades of the propeller carefully, until they are about ¹⁄₁₆″ in thickness.

6. Finish the propeller with fine sand-paper, No. 4-0. When complete, the blades should be less than ¹⁄₁₆″ in thickness, and the hub a little less than ⅛″ in thickness.

7. Sand the ends of the propeller round with fine sandpaper.

Propeller-Shaft

1. Make the propeller-shaft, O, from No. .020 music-wire. Make a ¼″ loop on one end of the shaft, and insert it in the propeller, as shown in the drawing, Plate XVII.

2. Make a small U-bend on the other end of the shaft, and cement the shaft securely to the propeller.

3. Place two medium-sized beads on the shaft, to cut down the friction between the bearing and the propeller.

Motor

1. Use a piece of ⅛″ flat rubber, 32″ long, forming two strands. Tie the ends in a square knot. There should be 1″ of slack when the rubber is in place.

2. Make the S-hook from No. .020 music-wire, to the shape shown in the drawing. The S-hook should be used with a winder.

Landing-Skid

1. Make the landing-skid from bamboo, ¹⁄₃₂″ x ¹⁄₃₂″ x 8″. Bend the lower curve by heating the bamboo over a candle flame or by steaming it.

2. Attach the skid by means of a brace, and ambroid to the under part of the front of the fuselage.

3. A landing-gear may be made from No. .016 music-wire, if you prefer.

Adjusting and Flying the "Junior Endurance Flyer"

1. Attach the wing to the motor-stick at a point close to the elevator.

2. After the plane has been assembled, allow the plane to glide from your hand, to test for balance and stability.

3. Wind the rubber around 200 times, and make further adjustments.

4. If the plane tries to climb too rapidly, set the wing a little farther back towards the elevator.

5. If it dives quickly, set the wing forward a little, and try the plane again.

6. When you are satisfied that your "Junior Flyer" glides evenly, wind the motor from 600 to a 1000 times for a trial flight.

7. When flying the plane indoors, especially during the winter months, you will want the plane to fly in a circular path. The size of the flying circle will depend on the size of the auditorium or hall.

8. When attaching the rudder to the fuselage, make a slight curve in the lower part of the rudder. This curved rudder will cause the plane to take a circular path while flying.

9. If the plane is to be flown outdoors, the rudder can be left straight.

Questions

1. What is the purpose of the elevator or stabilizer on a model airplane?

2. What makes this plane look like the long-neck goose?

3. Is there any advantage in making the ends of the propeller-blade round?

CHAPTER XIII

THE "BRYANT FLYER"

THE "Bryant Flyer" is a very good flyer, and capable of doing two minutes indoors, and from three to ten minutes outdoors. It was designed by Ronald Jacobson, a model-airplane enthusiast and student at the Bryant Junior High School, Minneapolis. The triangular shape of the elevator and the rudder are the main features of this model tractor plane.

Materials Required

(*A*) Fuselage, 1 pc, $\frac{1}{8}$" x $\frac{3}{16}$" x 17", balsa

(*B*) Wing, trailing edge, 1 pc, $\frac{1}{16}$" x $\frac{1}{8}$" x 20", balsa

(*B'*) Bearing, 1 pc, music-wire, .020, or flattened brad

(*C*) Wing, leading edge, 1 pc, $\frac{1}{16}$" x $\frac{1}{8}$" x 19", balsa

(*C'*) Rear hook, 1 pc, music-wire, .020 x $1\frac{1}{2}$" long

(*D*) Wing, tips, 2 pcs, $\frac{1}{16}$" x $\frac{1}{8}$" x $3\frac{3}{8}$", balsa

(*d*) Can, 1 pc, music-wire, .016 x $1\frac{1}{2}$" long

(*E*) Wing, ribs, 3 pcs, $\frac{1}{16}$" x $\frac{1}{8}$" x $3\frac{1}{4}$", balsa
S-hook, 1 pc, music-wire, .020 x $1\frac{1}{2}$" long

(*F*) Elevator, 1 back-piece, $\frac{1}{16}$" x $\frac{1}{8}$" x 6", balsa
1 pc, 5" x 7", Japanese tissue-paper

(*G*) Rudder, 1 vertical piece, $\frac{1}{16}$" x $\frac{1}{8}$" x 3", balsa
1 pc, 4" x 4", Japanese tissue-paper

(*H*) Wing-clips, 2 pcs, music-wire, .016 x $1\frac{1}{2}$" long

(*I*) Wing, covering, 1 pc, 4" x 21", Japanese tissue-paper

(*J*) Propeller, 1 pc, $\frac{3}{4}$" x $1\frac{1}{4}$" x 10", balsa

(*K*) Propeller-shaft, 1 pc, music-wire, .020 x 4" long

(*L*) Washer, 1 bead, medium size

The "Bryant Flyer"

(*M*) Motor, 1 pc, $\frac{1}{8}$" x 32" long, flat rubber band

(*S*) Wing, braces, 2 pcs, $\frac{1}{16}$" x $\frac{1}{8}$" x 5", balsa

Procedure

Fuselage

1. Cut a piece of balsa to the finished dimensions, $\frac{1}{8}$" x $\frac{3}{16}$" x 17", for the fuselage or motor-stick, *A*, Plate XVIII.

2. Split one end of the motor-stick, $\frac{1}{16}$" x $\frac{1}{16}$" x 3", as shown in the drawing. This section serves as the main support for the elevator.

Bearing

1. Make the front bearing, *B*, from a piece of No. .020 music-wire, or a flattened

THE BRYANT FLYER

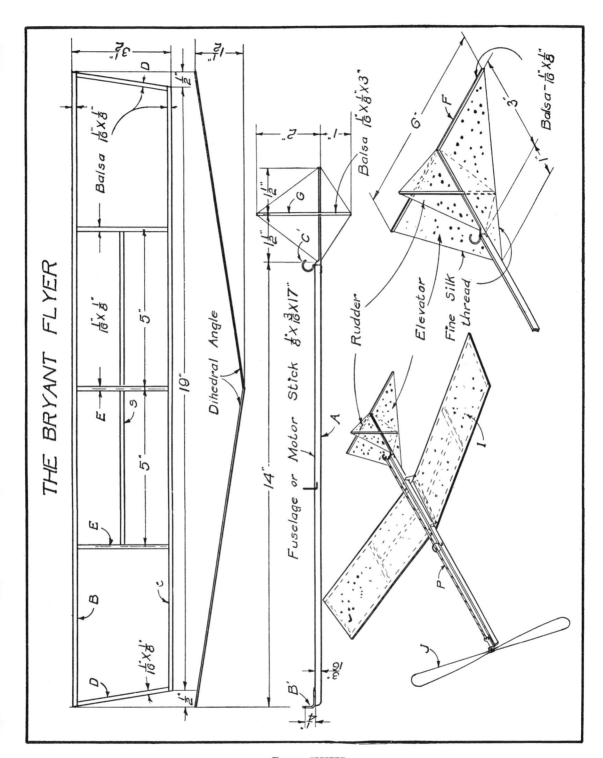

PLATE XVIII

brad. See Fig. 35. If you choose the brad, flatten a ⅝" brad with a hammer, and drill a hole in the metal with No. 70 drill or phonograph-needle.

2. Bend the bearing to an L-shape, and attach the bearing to the top front end of the fuselage with ambroid. A drop or two of ambroid will hold the bearing securely to the fuselage or motor-stick.

3. A bearing may be made from No. .020 music-wire, if you prefer. The wire bearing is easy to make, and works very nicely on this plane.

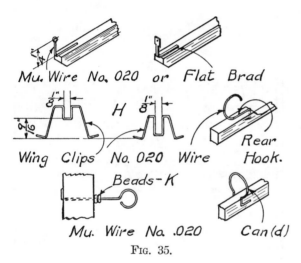

FIG. 35.

Rear Hook

1. Make the rear hook, C, from a piece of No. .020 music-wire. See Fig. 35. Bend the wire to the shape required with small round-nose pliers.

2. The rear hook should be made to hook in the rear end of the fuselage. Use ambroid, also, to fasten the rear hook.

Can

1. The can, d, is to prevent the fuselage from bending and breaking when the rubber is wound up.

2. Make the can from No. .016 music-wire, as shown in Fig. 35. The top part of the can should extend a little above the rubber motor.

Rudder

1. One feature of this plane is the rudder extending both above and below the fuselage. Make the vertical piece, G, from balsa, 1/16" x 1/8" x 3".

2. Cut a small notch in the fuselage, 1½" from the rear, and a small notch in the vertical piece.

3. Fasten the rudder-stick, G, to the rear of the fuselage with ambroid.

4. Use fine silk thread for the outline of the rudder.

Elevator

1. The elevator part of this plane is very simple to construct, but gives wonderful results. Make the rear piece, (F), 1/16" x 1/8" x 6", from balsa. Fasten this piece to the rear of the fuselage with ambroid or some good household cement.

2. Outline each side of the elevator with fine silk thread.

3. Cover the elevator and the rudder with Japanese tissue-paper. The tissue-paper should be ironed out smooth, before being attached to the elevator and the rudder.

4. Paint the under part of the elevator back piece and the back part of the fuselage with a thick banana-oil. Fasten the paper quickly before the oil dries.

5. Trim off the surplus tissue-paper with a razor-blade to a nice triangular shape.

6. The rudder should be covered in two separate sections. First, cut a piece of tissue-paper fitting the upper part of the rudder. Apply banana-oil to the vertical piece, the silk thread, and the side of the

rear of the fuselage. Attach the tissue-paper quickly before the banana-oil dries.

7. In like manner, the lower section of the rudder is covered with tissue-paper.

The Wing

1. Make the leading edge, C, $\frac{1}{16}''$ x $\frac{1}{8}''$ x 19'', and the trailing edge, B, $\frac{1}{16}''$ x $\frac{1}{8}''$ x 20'', from balsa wood. Make sure that these wing-spars are uniform in thickness and width.

2. Cut the wing-tips, D, $\frac{1}{16}''$ x $\frac{1}{8}''$ x $3\frac{3}{8}''$, to fit between the leading and trailing edges.

3. Cut the three ribs, E, to the finished dimensions, $\frac{1}{16}''$ x $\frac{1}{8}''$ x $3\frac{1}{4}''$, to fit between the wing-spars. See details in Plate XVIII.

4. Cut the two cross-braces, S, $\frac{1}{16}''$ x $\frac{1}{8}''$ x 5'', to fit between the ribs.

Wing-Form

1. A device such as a wing-form is very helpful in holding the wing in place, while bending the spars and assembling the different parts of the wing. See Fig. 33 and Fig. 34.

2. The wing-form can be made according to the dimensions shown in Fig. 34, from a piece of pine, 2'' x 4'' x 22''; or, it can be constructed from a piece of heavy cardboard.

3. The angle or the V-shaped opening in the form represents the dihedral angle that you will have in your wing.

4. Draw the outside outline of the wing on the form with a pencil.

5. Apply hot water or steam to the center portions of the two spars, and bend them to the V-shape of the form. Place the bent spars in the wing-form, accurately on the outline.

6. Cement the ribs and the wing tips between the leading edge and the trailing edge. In like manner, cement the braces, S, between the ribs.

7. Nail five or six wood cleats across the spars with small brads to hold the bent spars in place. See Fig. 33. When nailing the cleats, make sure that you barely touch the balsa spars with the pine cleats.

Wing-Clips

1. Make the two wing-clips from No. .020 music-wire. Bend the clips according to the dimensions and shapes given in Fig. 35. Use round-nose pliers in bending the clips. Be sure that the center opening of each clip is bent to fit the fuselage or motor-stick tightly.

2. The higher clip is placed in the rear, and is $\frac{9}{16}''$ higher than the front clip. The difference in the heights of the two clips gives the wing an upward slant, to make the plane climb. This upward slant is known as the angle of incidence, and should be checked carefully.

3. When you are satisfied that your clips are of the right size and shape, cement them exactly in the center of the wing spars.

4. Take a piece of Japanese tissue-paper, $3\frac{3}{4}''$ x 21'', and iron it out so that it will be perfectly smooth.

5. Cut the paper to fit around the wing-clips.

6. Paint the top of the spars, ribs, and tips with thick banana-oil. Paint only a part of the wing at a time, and attach the paper to the wing, starting at the center rib and working out to the tips of the wing. Work carefully when applying the banana-oil and attaching the paper, to insure smoothness of paper and a neat job. A smooth surface of the wing is very essential to good flying.

7. When the wing is completely covered, trim the surplus paper with a razor-blade.

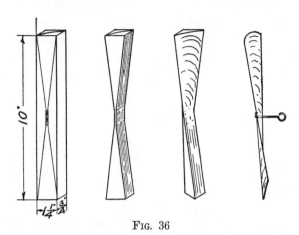

FIG. 36

Propeller

1. Make the propeller for the "Bryant Flyer" from balsa wood, 1/4" x 1 1/4" x 10". Mark the block by drawing fine lines diagonally on one flat surface. See Fig. 36.

2. Make a small hole at the intersection of the diagonal lines, at the exact center of the block, with a pin or No. .020 music-wire.

3. Carve the block to the diagonal lines, leaving the center part of the block 3/16" thick. This part is left thicker, to prevent breaking while carving the blades of the propeller.

4. Draw the end diagonal lines, to show the end shape and the pitch of the propeller. Make sure that the two end diagonal lines run in opposite directions.

5. Carve out the blades of the propeller carefully, until they are about 1/16" in thickness. Finish the propeller with fine sandpaper. When complete, the blades should be less than 1/16" in thickness, and the hub a little less than 1/8" in thickness. Sand the ends of the propeller round with fine sandpaper, No. 4-0.

Propeller-Shaft

1. Make the propeller-shaft, K, Fig. 35, from No. .020 music-wire.

2. Make a 5/16" loop on one end of the shaft, and insert the shaft in the propeller, as shown in the drawing.

3. Make a small U-bend on the other end of the shaft, and cement the shaft securely to the propeller.

4. Place a medium-sized bead on the shaft, to cut down the friction between the bearing and the propeller.

5. An S-hook is essential when using a winder in winding the motor of your plane. Make the S-hook from No. .020 music-wire.

Adjusting and Flying the "Bryant Flyer"

1. Attach the wing to the motor-stick at a point close to the elevator.

2. After the plane has been assembled, allow the plane to glide from your hand, to test the balance.

3. Wind the rubber 100 or 200 turns, and make further adjustments.

4. If the plane climbs too rapidly, set the wing a little farther back towards the elevator.

5. If it dives quickly, set the wing forward a little, and try the plane again.

6. When you are satisfied that your "Bryant Flyer" glides and flies evenly, wind the motor 500 to 1000 times for a trial flight.

7. When flying the plane indoors, especially during the winter months, you will want the plane to fly in a circular path. When attaching the rudder to the fuselage, make a slight curve in the rudder. This curved rudder will cause the plane to take a circular path while flying. The size of the flying circle will depend on the size of the auditorium or hall.

8. However, if the plane is to be flown outdoors, the rudder may be left straight.

Questions

1. What is the difference between a motor-boat propeller and an airplane propeller?

2. You will find that a model plane made from pine will remain in the air but a short time. Why?

3. Japanese tissue-paper is recommended for covering model airplanes. Why?

4. What is meant by the dihedral angle?

5. What is meant by the fuselage or motor-stick?

CHAPTER XIV

THE "TWIN SKIIPLANE" OR "SEAPLANE"

THE "Twin Skiiplane" or "Seaplane" is a novelty twin pusher that will fly over land, water, or snow. It can take off from the snow on a mild winter day as well as from the water or the land on a fine spring or summer day. Thus, if you are near a body of water, slip on your pontoons, and let your famous "Twin" take a flight over the lake or sea.

Or, again, if you want to fly your model in a contest on land, you can add a landing-gear of your own invention.

The skiis on your plane will work very well, and will be most appropriate for a flight on a mild winter day. See Fig. 37.

The "Twin Skiiplane" or "Seaplane" will, however, fly very well without a landing-gear, skiis, or pontoons.

The "Twin Skiiplane" or "Seaplane"

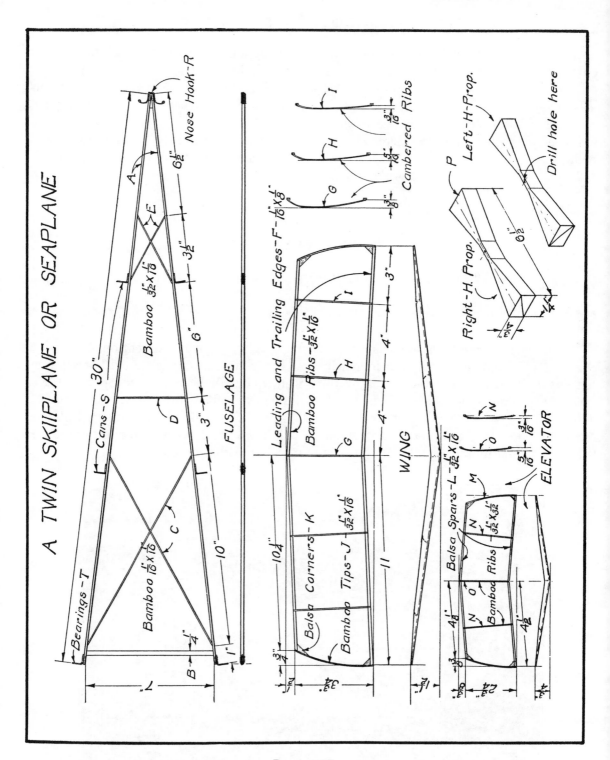

A TWIN SKIPLANE OR SEAPLANE

PLATE XIX

88

You will surely get a lot of pleasure in making and flying this novelty twin model plane.

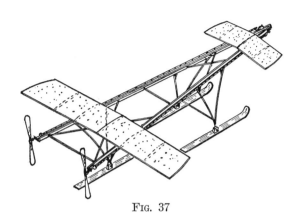

FIG. 37

Materials Required

Fuselage

(A) Beams, 2 pcs, $\frac{3}{32}$" x $\frac{3}{16}$" x 30", balsa
(B) Back-brace, 1 pc, $\frac{3}{32}$" x $\frac{1}{4}$" x 7", balsa
(C) Back cross-braces, 2 pcs, $\frac{1}{16}$" x $\frac{1}{16}$" x 13", bamboo
(D) Center-brace, 1 pc, $\frac{1}{32}$" x $\frac{1}{16}$" x 5", bamboo
(E) Front cross-braces, 2 pcs, $\frac{1}{32}$" x $\frac{1}{16}$" x $5\frac{1}{2}$", bamboo
(R) Nose-hook, 1 pc, music-wire, .025 x 5" long
(S) Cans, 4 pcs, music-wire, .025 x 3" long
(T) Bearings, 2 nails, safety-pins, or music-wire, .025

Wing

(F-1) Leading edge, 1 pc, $\frac{1}{16}$" x $\frac{1}{8}$" x $20\frac{1}{2}$", balsa
(F-2) Trailing edge, 1 pc, $\frac{1}{16}$" x $\frac{1}{8}$" x 22", balsa
(G, H, I) Ribs, 5 pcs, $\frac{3}{64}$" x $\frac{1}{16}$" x 4", bamboo
(J) Tips, 2 pcs, $\frac{1}{32}$" x $\frac{1}{16}$" x 4", bamboo
(K) Corner-braces, 4 pcs, $\frac{1}{16}$" x $\frac{1}{4}$" x $\frac{3}{8}$", balsa
Covering, 1 pc, 4" x 23", Japanese tissue-paper

Elevator

(L-1) Leading edge, 1 pc, $\frac{1}{32}$" x $\frac{1}{16}$" x $8\frac{1}{4}$", balsa
(L-2) Trailing edge, 1 pc, $\frac{1}{32}$" x $\frac{1}{16}$" x 9", balsa
(M) Wing-tips, 2 pcs, $\frac{1}{32}$" x $\frac{3}{32}$" x 3" bamboo
(N, O) Ribs, 3 pcs, $\frac{1}{32}$" x $\frac{1}{32}$" x 3", bamboo
Covering, 1 pc, 3" x 10", Japanese tissue-paper

Power-Plant

(P) Propeller, 2 pcs, $\frac{3}{4}$" x $1\frac{1}{4}$" x $6\frac{1}{2}$", balsa
(Q) Propeller-shaft, 2 pcs, music-wire, .025 x 5" long
Washers, 4, light brass
S-hooks, 2 pcs, music-wire, .025 x 5" long
Motor, 2 pcs, $\frac{1}{8}$" x 20' 0", flat rubber band
Thick banana-oil, 2 oz.
Light dope, 2 oz.
Ambroid cement, 2 oz.

Procedure

Fuselage

1. Make the two beams of the fuselage, A, Plate XIX, from balsa, $\frac{3}{32}$" x $\frac{3}{16}$" x 30".

2. On a piece of wrapping-paper or drawing-paper lay out a full-sized drawing of the fuselage or framework.

3. Cut the angle on the front end of each beam, A, according to the angle given in your full-size drawing, from the dimensions given in Plate XIX.

4. Place your full-size drawing on a box or large board, and construct the framework or fuselage on top of the drawing.

5. Cut out a piece of balsa, $\frac{3}{32}$" x $\frac{1}{4}$" x 7", for the rear brace, B, and cut the end angles of this piece according to the angles shown in your full-sized drawing.

6. Make the nose-hook, R, from No. .025 music-wire. Follow the dimensions and

general shape of the nose-hook given in Fig. 38.

7. Fit the nose-hook over the two cut beams before the fuselage is assembled in order to get a good fit.

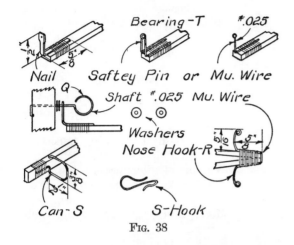

Fig. 38

8. Make the two bearings from safety-pins, flattened nails, or No. .025 music-wire. All three types of bearing have been used with good results by the boys in my shop. A small safety-pin makes a very satisfactory bearing for this type of plane. However, see 38, and take your choice.

9. Fasten the bearings to the rear ends of the beams with ambroid and fine silk thread.

10. Assemble the framework of your plane next. Dip the front ends of the beams in ambroid, and fasten these pieces together by inserting the nose-hook forming the V-shaped front end. Wind fine silk thread around nose-hook and beams, as shown in Fig. 38.

11. Fasten the rear brace, B, to the beams, 3/8″ from the rear ends with ambroid.

12. Fasten the fuselage or framework to a box or a board when assembling the parts. This can be done by inserting small brads in the board on each side of the beams to keep them in place.

13. Ambroid the cross-braces, C and E, and the middle brace, D, in their proper places. See Plate XIX for correct dimensions and spacing of these parts.

14. Place the two cans, S, one on the outside of each beam, equal distances apart. Fasten these cans or guides with ambroid and fine silk thread. Make sure that the centers of the cans, the bearings, and the loop of the nose-hook are in perfect line.

Wing

1. Make the leading edge of the wing, F-1, to the finished dimensions, 1/16″ x 1/8″ x 20½″, from balsa. Make the trailing edge, F-2, to the finished dimensions, 1/16″ x 1/8″ x 22″ from balsa. Be sure that these two spars are of uniform thickness and width.

2. Cut the wing-tips, J, 1/32″ x 1/16″ x 4″, from bamboo. In like manner, prepare the ribs, G, H, I, 3/64″ x 1/16″ x 4″, from bamboo also.

3. Before we go any further it will be necessary to build a form of some kind to hold the wing in place and to the proper dihedral angle, while assembling. Two boards, ½″ x 5″ x 24″, with blocks nailed to the ends, raising the end 1½″, will serve the purpose of a form very nicely. This form should be nailed solid to some discarded piece of lumber or a box.

4. Draw the outline with a pencil on the form. Make sure that the tips are of the curve shown in the drawing, Plate XIX. Steam the center portions of the leading and trailing edges and bend them at the exact center.

5. The wing-spars can be held in place in the form by nailing a number of pine cleats across the spars with small brads.

See Fig. 33. Be sure that the cleats barely touch the wing spars when nailing.

6. Fasten the wing-tips, *J*, next. Steam the tips to the curve shown in your outline, and fasten to the leading and trailing edges with ambroid. Nail a number of small brads in the form on each side of the curve to hold the tips in place until the ambroid is dry.

7. Cement the four balsa corner-blocks, *K*, next. These small blocks are very light, but are a great help in keeping the wing the right shape.

8. Make a pine template or form for each of the ribs, *G*, *H*, and *I*. These templates may be placed in the wing where the ribs are to be located.

9. Steam the ribs, one at a time, and bend them over the forms in their proper places and to the proper shape. When you are satisfied with position and shape, ambroid each rib to the leading and trailing edges, as shown in the drawing, Plate XIX.

10. Leave the wing to dry in the form, while you proceed to make the elevator.

Elevator

1. The elevator in this plane is a small wing, built in exactly the same manner as the main wing. Make the leading edge, *L*, to the finished dimensions, $\frac{1}{32}''$ x $\frac{1}{16}''$ x $8\frac{1}{4}''$, and the trailing edge, *L-2*, to the finished dimensions, $\frac{1}{32}''$ x $\frac{1}{16}''$ x 9'', from balsa. Be sure that these pieces are of uniform thickness and width.

2. Cut the tips, *M*, $\frac{1}{32}''$ x $\frac{1}{16}''$ x 3'', from bamboo.

3. In like manner, prepare the ribs, *O* and *N*, $\frac{1}{32}''$ x $\frac{1}{32}''$ x 3'', from bamboo also.

4. Prepare a form like the one made for the main wing; or, a solid block carved out to the shape of your elevator, can be used.

5. Assemble the elevator in the very same manner in which you assembled the main wing.

Covering Wing and Elevator

1. Cover the wing and the elevator with Japanese tissue-paper. A heavy banana-oil is used to fasten the paper. Start covering the wing by painting the center rib with heavy banana-oil, and start fastening your paper at this point. Allow this part to dry before proceeding to the next rib.

2. Paint the next rib, and fasten the paper, pulling the paper tight lengthwise to produce a neat job between sections. Proceed section by section, until the whole wing is covered. Fasten the paper to the trailing and leading edges next.

3. Cover the under part of the entire wing neatly as a final touch.

4. Cover the elevator exactly as you covered the main wing.

Propellers

1. The propellers are carved from balsa blocks, $\frac{3}{4}''$ x $1\frac{1}{4}''$ x $6\frac{1}{2}''$ in size. Mark each block by drawing fine lines diagonally on one flat surface. Make a small hole at the intersection of the lines, or at the exact center of each block, with the No. .025 music-wire.

2. Carve each block to the diagonal lines, leaving the center $\frac{3}{16}''$ thick. This part is left thicker, to prevent breaking while carving the blades.

3. Draw the end diagonal lines next. Place the two blocks, side by side, and draw the lines so that they run in opposite directions. One propeller is right-handed, and the other is left-handed. See Plate XIX.

4. Carve out the blades, until they taper gradually from the thickness of the hub at the center to $\frac{1}{16}''$ or less at the tips.

5. With fine sandpaper, sand the blades, so that the front of each is slightly rounded, and the rear convex.

6. Round the ends with fine sandpaper. Be sure the four ends are exactly the same shape.

7. The hub of each propeller should be about $\frac{3}{8}''$ thick.

8. Give each propeller three coats of banana-oil, and sand lightly between coats.

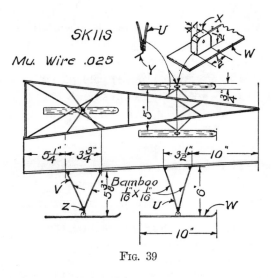

Fig. 39

Propeller-Shafts

1. Make the propeller-shafts, Q, from No. .026 music-wire, See Fig. 38. Make a $\frac{5}{16}''$ loop on one end of each shaft, to receive one end of the rubber motor, and insert the other end of the shaft in the propeller.

2. Make a small U-bend on the opposite end of each shaft, and cement the shafts securely to the propellers.

3. Place two thin brass washers on each shaft, to cut down the friction between the bearings and the propellers.

Motor

1. Use six or seven strands of $\frac{1}{8}''$ flat rubber band, or about 20 feet, for each motor. About $1\frac{1}{2}''$ slack should be allowed for each motor before winding.

2. Make two S-hooks from No. .025 music-wire, to the shape shown in Fig. 38. The S-hooks are used in winding the motors with a winder.

Adjusting and Flying the "Twin Skiiplane" or "Seaplane"

1. Attach the wing to the fuselage with rubber bands, about $4''$ or $5''$ from the propellers.

2. Fasten the elevator to the front end of the fuselage with a strong rubber band. See Fig. 39. It is very essential that the wing and the elevator are held in position securely, after the best flying adjustments have been determined.

3. Thread the motors through the cans, attaching one end of each motor to its propeller-shaft, and the other end to the nose-hook by means of the S-hook.

4. Glide the model, by launching it level with your shoulder, and watch for results. If the nose rises and the plane stalls before landing, the wings should be moved a little to the rear.

5. Adjust the wings until you have discovered the best adjustment for a long even glide.

6. For a trial flight, wind each motor about 200 times with a winder of the egg-beater type.

7. The owner of the plane should always have a good reliable assistant to help in winding the motors. With the assistant holding the propellers at the hubs, and the same time holding the frame, the pilot steps back about 5 feet, stretching the rubber before winding it. More turns can be

made on each motor by stretching the rubber in this manner.

8. After winding each motor, about 200 or 300 times in opposite directions, launch the plane by holding it by the propellers, with its nose pointing up. If the model is adjusted right, it should take off quickly, and travel a good distance on 300 turns.

9. If the plane climbs steeply and stalls, it will be necessary to move the wings back slightly for a second flight. The wings are well adjusted if the plane stalls occasionally, and climbs well between stalls.

10. For an official flight or a long flight wind the motors 800 to 1000 turns. Be sure to stretch the rubber well before winding.

11. By releasing the plane with a slight push, it will begin to rise rapidly; and, as it gains altitude, it will travel fast and a long distance.

Questions

1. What will happen if you wind the two propellers in the same direction?

2. Why should you stretch the rubber before winding the motors?

3. Why should you not use balsa for the cross-braces instead of bamboo?

4. What would happen if you left off the cans from your "Twin" pusher?

CHAPTER XV

THE "SKY SPEED TWIN"

HERE, BOYS, is the endurance Speed King of the air. It can make a flight up in the clouds of 12 minutes or more. At a recent contest, the "Sky Speed Twin" made a record flight of 12 minutes. It flew so far and so high, that it required a lot of energy and speed for the pilot to keep in sight of the plane.

The twin-pusher type of plane is still the best and most reliable outdoor model made. If you are careful in following the directions, you can produce a real flying model.

Before building the "Sky Speed Twin," make sure that you have a suitable hangar or box in which to keep the parts during the period of construction.

Materials Required

Fuselage

(A-1) Beams, 2 pcs, 3⁄16″ x 5⁄16″ x 42″, balsa

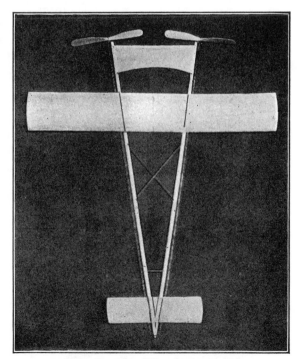

FIG. 40. The "Sky Speed Twin"

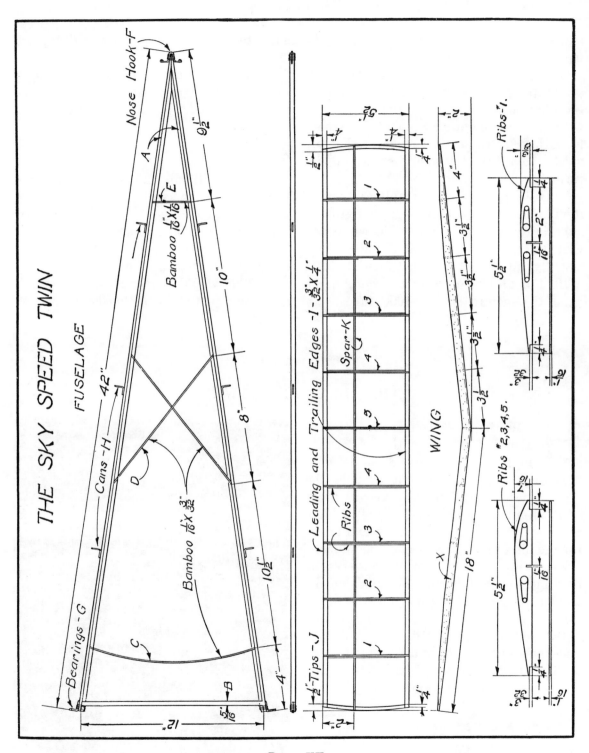

THE SKY SPEED TWIN

PLATE XX

94

(*A-2*) Beams, 2 pcs, ⅛" x ³⁄₁₆" x 42", balsa
(*B*) Back-brace, 1 pc, ³⁄₃₂" x ⁵⁄₁₆" x 12", balsa
(*C*) Back tail-brace, 1 pc, ¹⁄₁₆" x ³⁄₃₂" x 12½", bamboo
(*D*) Cross-brace, 2 pcs, ¹⁄₁₆" x ³⁄₃₂" x 11", bamboo
(*E*) Front-brace, 1 pc, ¹⁄₁₆" x ¹⁄₁₆" x 3", bamboo
(*F*) Nose-hook, 1 pc, music-wire, .035 x 6" long
(*G*) Bearings, 2 pcs, aluminum, 22-gage, or 2 safety-pins, or ¾" brads
(*H*) Cans, 6 pcs, music-wire, .020 x 3" long

Wing

(*I*) Leading and trailing edges, 2 pcs, ³⁄₃₂" x ¼" x 36", balsa
(*J*) Tips, 2 pcs, ³⁄₃₂" x ½" x 5", balsa
(*K*) Middle spar, 1 pc, ¹⁄₁₆" x ³⁄₁₆" x 36", balsa
Rib No. 1, 2 pcs, ¹⁄₁₆" x ⁷⁄₁₆" x 5½", balsa
Ribs Nos. 2, 3, 4, 5, 7 pcs, ¹⁄₁₆" x ⅜" x 5½", balsa
(*X*) Covering, 1 pc, 4" x 138", Japanese tissue-paper
(*Y*) Back fuselage cover, 1 pc, 4" x 13", Japanese tissue-paper

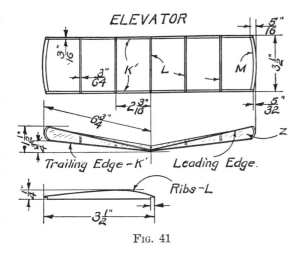

ELEVATOR

Trailing Edge – *K'*   Leading Edge.

Ribs – *L*

FIG. 41

Elevator

(*K-1*) Leading and trailing edges, 2 pcs, ³⁄₃₂" x ³⁄₁₆" x 13½", balsa

(*L*) Ribs, 5 pcs, ³⁄₆₄" x ¼" x 3¼", balsa
(*M*) Tips, 2 pcs, ³⁄₆₄" x ⁵⁄₁₆" x 3¼", balsa
(*Z*) Covering, 1 pc, 4" x 14", Japanese tissue-paper

Propellers

(*O*) Washers, 4, light brass
(*P*) Propellers, 2 pcs, ¾" x 1½" x 12", balsa
(*Q*) Propeller-shaft, 2 pcs, music-wire, .035 x 5" long
S-hooks, 2 pcs, music-wire, .035 x5" long
Motor, 2 pcs, ⅛" x 36' 0" long, flat rubber band
Spaghetti tube, for propeller-shaft, 1 pc, 6" long
Thick banana-oil, 2 oz.
Light dope, 2 oz.
Ambroid cement, 2 oz.

Procedure

Fuselage

1. Each beam of the fuselage is built from two pieces of balsa. See Plate XX. One piece, *A-1*, is ³⁄₁₆" x ⁵⁄₁₆" x 42", when finished, and the other, *A-2*, is ⅛" x ³⁄₁₆"

2. Fasten piece *A-2* to the center of piece *A-1* with ambroid. Work fast, so that the ambroid will not dry too quickly. A few small brads may be inserted in *A-2*, to hold the two pieces together until the ambroid sets. After the ambroid is dry, remove the brads to lessen the weight of the beams.

3. On a piece of wrapping-paper or drawing-paper, lay out a full-sized drawing of the fuselage or framework.

4. Cut the front end of the beams according to the angle shown on your drawing, as laid out from the dimensions given in Plate XX.

5. The fuselage can then be easily constructed on top of this accurate drawing on a work-bench or a large board.

6. Cut out a piece of balsa, ³⁄₃₂" x ⁵⁄₁₆" x 12", for the rear brace, *B*. Cut the end

angle of this piece according to the angle given in your full-sized drawing.

7. Make the nose-hook, *F*, from No. .035 music-wire. Follow the dimensions and general shape as given in Fig. 42. Fit the nose-hook over the two beams before the fuselage is assembled, in order to get a good fit.

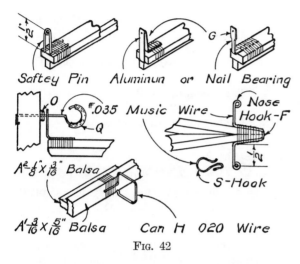

FIG. 42

8. Make the two bearings from safety-pins, aluminum, or flattened brads. All three types of bearing have been used with good results by the boys here. The medium-sized safety-pin makes an ideal bearing for this type of plane. See Fig. 42, and take your choice.

9. Fasten each bearing to the rear end of its beam with ambroid and fine silk thread.

10. Assemble your fuselage by first dipping the front ends of the beams in ambroid. Fasten these pieces together by inserting the nose-hook over them, forming the V-frame. Wind fine silk thread around nose-hook and ends of beams. See Fig. 42.

11. Fasten the rear brace, *B*, to the beams with ambroid ½″ from the ends. It

is well to fasten the frame to a bench or board when assembling the fuselage parts. This can be done by inserting small brads in the board on each side of each beam, to keep them in place.

12. Fasten the rear bamboo tail-piece, *C*, to the beams with ambroid.

13. Ambroid the cross-braces, *D*, and the brace, *E*, in their proper places. See Plate XX for correct dimensions.

14. Place the three "cans" on the outside of each beam, equal distances apart. Fasten these cans or guides with ambroid and fine silk thread. Make sure that the centers of the cans, the bearings, and the loop of the nose-hook are in perfect line.

The Wing

1. Make the leading and trailing edges of the wing, *I*, from balsa, to the finished dimensions, ³⁄₃₂″ x ¼″ x 35½″. Be sure that these spars are of uniform thickness and width.

2. Cut the two tips, *J*, to a curved shape from balsa pieces, ³⁄₃₂″ x ½″ x 5″.

3. Cut the center-brace spar, *K*, from balsa, to the finished dimensions, ¹⁄₁₆″ x ³⁄₁₆″ x 36″.

4. Make the two No. 1 ribs, ¹⁄₁₆″ x ⁷⁄₁₆″ x 5½″, from balsa. Make a template or pattern of the No. 1 ribs out of cardboard or drawing-paper before shaping. See Plate XX for details.

5. Trace around the pattern on the block, and shape the ribs to the proper shape with a sharp razor-blade.

6. In like manner, make a pattern for ribs Nos. 2, 3, 4, and 5, and carve the ribs. See detail drawing, Plate XX.

Assembling the Wing

1. In order to hold your wing at the proper dihedral angle while assembling, it

is necessary to use a form. Two boards, ¾" x 6" x 38", with a block nailed to the ends, raising the ends 2", will serve the purpose very nicely. This form should be nailed solid to some discarded piece of lumber or box.

2. Steam the center portions of the leading and the trailing edges, and bend them at the exact center. The edges can be held in place in the form by nailing a number of pine cleats across the spars with small brads. See Fig. 33.

3. Fasten the wing-tips, J, between the leading and trailing edges with ambroid.

4. Fasten the two No. 1 ribs to the leading and trailing edges with ambroid also.

5. In like manner, ambroid all the ribs in their respective places, equal distances apart.

6. When the ribs and tips are completely dried, remove the assembled fuselage from the form, and insert the spar, K, in the notches of the ribs on the rear of the wing.

7. Round the edges of leading and trailing edges and the wing-tips with fine sandpaper.

8. The wing is now ready to be covered with Japanese tissue-paper. But we will proceed to complete the elevator, first, and then do all the covering at the same time. You might leave your wing in the form while you are working on the elevator.

Elevator

1. The leading and trailing edges of the elevator, K-1, are made from balsa, and are of the same size; that is, ³⁄₃₂" x ³⁄₁₆" x 13½", finished dimensions.

2. Cut the two tips, M, to a curved shape from balsa pieces, ³⁄₃₂" x ⁵⁄₁₆" x 3¼".

3. Make the five ribs, L, from balsa pieces, ³⁄₆₄ x ¼" x 3¼". Make a full-sized template from cardboard or drawing-pa-

per, and shape all the five ribs from this pattern. Cut the ribs to the finished shape with a sharp razor-blade.

Elevator-Form

1. It is necessary to make a form of some kind to hold the parts while assembling the elevator, and in order to insure the proper angle of incidence shown in the drawing, Fig. 41. Make a form from a solid piece of pine, or from cardboard. Note that the ends of the trailing edge are ¾" higher than the center of the spar, and the ends of the leading edge are 1½" higher than the center of the leading edge. After the form has been carefully contructed, it becomes a simple job to assemble the elevator properly.

2. Draw the outside outline of the elevator on the form with a pencil. Apply hot water or steam to the center portions of the two spars, and bend them to the V-shape indicated.

3. Place the bent spars in the form on the outline, and nail four or five pine cleats across the spars with small brads to hold the edges in place.

4. Fasten the tips between the leading and trailing edges at the extreme ends of the elevator with ambroid.

5. Fasten the five ribs to the leading and trailing edges, equal distances apart. See Fig. 41.

Covering Wing and Elevator

1. Cover the wing, elevator, and tailpiece with Japanese tissue-paper, using a heavy banana-oil to fasten the paper. The wing and elevator may be covered with preshrunk Japanese silk tissue-paper, if preferred. This type of paper, having been shrunk, does not require dope after it is fastened to the plane.

2. We shall use Japanese tissue-paper on this plane. Start covering the wing by painting the center rib with heavy banana-oil, and start fastening your paper at this point. Allow this part to dry before going to the next rib.

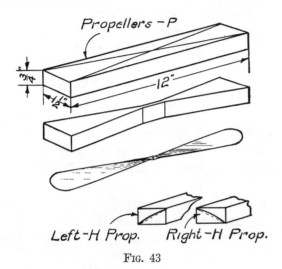

FIG. 43

3. Paint the next rib, and fasten the paper, pulling the paper tight lengthwise to produce a neat job betwen sections. Proceed section by section until the whole wing is covered. Cover the under part of the wing also.

4. When the entire wing is covered, give it a medium coat of airplane dope.

5. Cover the elevator the same way you covered the wing, by starting at the center rib, and working to both sides.

6. Cover the tail with Japanese tissue-paper also.

Propellers

1. Carve the propellers from balsa blocks, ¾" x 1½" x 12". See Fig. 43. Mark each block by drawing fine lines diagonally on one flat surface. Make a small hole at the intersection of the lines, or at the exact center of each block, with a pin or No. .035 music-wire.

2. Carve each block to the diagonal lines, leaving the center part ¾₆" thick. This part is left thicker, in order to prevent breaking while carving the blades.

3. Draw the end diagonal lines next. Place the two blocks, side by side, and draw a diagonal line on the end of each block, so that the diagonals run in opposite directions. See Fig. 43. One propeller is right-handed, and the other is left-handed.

4. Carve out the blades of the propellers until they taper gradually, from the thickness of the hub at the center to ¹⁄₁₆" or less at the tips.

5. With fine sandpaper, sand each blade so that the front is slightly rounded, and the rear is convex.

6. Round off the four propeller-tips with fine sandpaper. Be sure they are all exactly the same shape. The hub of each propeller should be about ⁷⁄₁₆" thick.

7. Balance your propellers very carefully before attaching them to the plane.

8. Give each propeller three coats of banana-oil, and sand lightly between coats.

Propeller-Shafts

1. Make the propeller-shafts, Q, from No. .035 music-wire. See Fig. 42. Make a ⅜" loop on one end of the shaft to receive one end of the rubber motor, and insert the other end of the shaft in the propeller.

2. Make a small V-bend on the opposite end of each shaft, and cement the shafts securely to the propellers.

3. Place two thin brass washers on each shaft, to cut down the friction between the bearings and the propellers.

Motor

1. Use 9 strands, or about 36 feet, of ⅛" flat rubber for each motor. There should

be about 2″ slack in each motor before winding.

2. Make two S-hooks from No. .035 music-wire, of the shape shown in Fig. 42. The S-hooks are used in winding the motors with a winder.

Adjusting and Flying the "Sky Speed Twin"

1. Attach the wing to the fuselage with ⅛″ rubber bands, 7″ or 8″ from the propellers. See Fig. 40.

2. Fasten the elevator to the front end of the fuselage with a strong rubber band; say, ⅛″ flat rubber. It is very essential that the wing and elevator be held securely in position after the best flying adjustment has been determined.

3. Thread the motors through the cans, attaching one end of each to its propeller-shaft, and the other ends to the nose-hook by means of the S-hook.

4. Glide the model by launching it, level with your shoulders, and watch for results. If the nose rises and the plane stalls before landing, the wings should be moved a little to the rear.

5. Adjust the wings until you have discovered the best adjustment for a long even glide.

6. For a trial flight, wind each motor about 500 times with a winder of the egg-beater type. The flier should always have a good reliable assistant to help in winding the motors. With the assistant holding the propellers at the hubs, and at the same time holding the frame, the pilot steps back about 6 feet, stretching the rubber before winding it. More turns can be made on each motor by stretching the rubber in this manner.

7. After winding each motor about 500 turns, in opposite directions, launch the plane by holding it by the two propellers, with its nose pointing up. If adjusted properly, the plane should take off quickly, and travel a good distance on 500 turns.

8. If the plane climbs steeply and stalls, it will be necessary to move the wings back slightly for a second flight. The wings are well adjusted if the plane stalls occasionally, and climbs well between stalls.

9. For an official flight, wind the motors 1200 to 1500 turns. Be sure to stretch the rubber well before winding. Release the plane with a slight push; it will begin to rise rapidly; and, as it gains altitude, it will travel quite fast. This plane will travel well over a mile on a straight course; so it is well to have a bicycle at hand, to assist in keeping the plane in sight.

Questions

1. What makes this type of plane a good flyer?

2. Why should the wing of an airplane be covered with dope?

3. Why should a twin pusher be launched against the wind?

4. What is a "cambered" wing?

Chapter XVI

THE "WHITE BIRD"

OW WOULD you like to make a model airplane like some of the man-sized commercial airplanes flying about you each day? The "White Bird" is not a duplication of any special make of plane, but it is a "real" model airplane of the popular cabin type that flies high and flies well for long distance flights. If built lightly, according to the drawings, you will produce an airplane that you will be proud of. This is a model that will give you endless pleasure, flying it outdoors in the wide open spaces, or indoors in your school auditorium, or in the neighborhood gymnasium or hall.

Materials Required

Fuselage

(A) Nose, 1 pc, $\frac{3}{4}$" x $2\frac{7}{8}$" x $2\frac{7}{8}$", balsa
(B) Section, 1 pc, $\frac{3}{16}$" x $2\frac{7}{8}$" x $2\frac{7}{8}$", balsa
(C) Section, 1 pc, $\frac{3}{32}$" x $3\frac{3}{16}$" x $3\frac{5}{8}$", balsa
(D) Section, 1 pc, $\frac{3}{32}$" x $3\frac{1}{4}$" x $3\frac{3}{4}$", balsa
(E) Section, 1 pc, $\frac{3}{32}$" x $3\frac{1}{16}$" x $3\frac{1}{2}$", balsa
(F) Section, 1 pc, $\frac{3}{32}$" x $1\frac{15}{16}$" x $2\frac{3}{8}$", balsa
(G) Tail-piece, 1 pc, $\frac{1}{2}$" x $\frac{3}{4}$" x $\frac{3}{4}$", balsa
(H) Longerons, 4 pcs, $\frac{3}{32}$" x $\frac{5}{32}$" x 25", balsa
(I) Motor-stick, 1 pc, $\frac{1}{4}$" diameter x 22", dowel-rod, pine
Covering, 3 pcs. 12" x 38", Japanese tissue-paper

Stabilizer

(K-1) Spar, 1 pc, $\frac{1}{16}$" x $\frac{1}{16}$" x $10\frac{1}{2}$", bamboo
(K-2) Edges, 2 pcs, $\frac{3}{64}$" x $\frac{1}{16}$" x 15", bamboo
(K-3) Ribs, 2 pcs, $\frac{3}{64}$" x $\frac{1}{16}$" x $3\frac{1}{2}$", bamboo

Elevator

(L-1) Spars, 2 pcs, $\frac{1}{16}$" x $\frac{1}{16}$" x 6", bamboo
(L-2) Edges, 2 pcs, $\frac{3}{64}$" x $\frac{1}{16}$" x 10", bamboo
(L-3) Ribs, 2 pcs, $\frac{3}{64}$" x $\frac{1}{16}$" x 2", bamboo

Fin and Rudder

(M-1) Vertical piece, 1 pc, $\frac{1}{16}$" x $\frac{1}{16}$" x $3\frac{3}{8}$", bamboo

FIG. 44. The frame of the "White Bird" before the covering is applied

(*M-2*) Edges, 1 pc, 3/64″ x 1/16″ x 6″, bamboo
(*M-3*) Lower edge, 1 pc, 3/64″ x 1/16″ x 5″, bamboo
(*N-1*) Vertical piece, 1 pc, 1/16″ x 1/16″ x 4″, bamboo
(*N-2*) Edges, 1 pc, 3/64″ x 1/16″ x 10″, bamboo

Wing

(*O*) Ribs, 13 pcs, 3/32″ x 5/8″ x 6 1/4″, balsa
(*P*) Top spars, 2 pcs, 1/8″ x 1/4″ x 36″, balsa
(*Q*) Leading edge, 1 pc, 1/8″ x 3/16″ x 36″, balsa
(*Q*) Trailing edge, 1 pc, 1/8″ x 3/16″ x 36″, balsa
Covering, 3 pcs, 8″ x 40″, Japanese tissue-paper

Power-Plant

(*X*) Propeller, 1 pc, 7/8″ x 1 3/4″ x 10″, balsa
(*e*) Propeller-shaft, 1 pc, bicycle-spoke, or commercial ball-bearing shaft
(*e′*) Shaft-bearing, 1 pc, bicycle-bearing, or commercial ball-bearing
(*f*) Motor, 1/8″ flat rubber band, 16″ strands, or 26′0″
(*g*) Rear hook, 1 pc, music-wire, .035 x 5″ long
Washers, 2, light brass

Chassis

(*R*) Wing-braces, 4 pcs, 3/32″ x 1/4″ x 7 1/4″, balsa
(*S*) Chassis-braces, 2 pcs, 3/32″ x 1/4″ x 5 1/2″, balsa
(*T*) Chassis-braces, 2 pcs, 3/32″ x 1/4″ x 5 3/4″, balsa
(*U*) Cross-braces, 2 pcs, 3/32″ x 1/4″ x 7 1/2″, balsa
(*W*) Wheels, 2 pcs, 1/4″ thick x 2 1/2″ diameter, balsa
(*a, b*) Tube-fittings, 6 pcs, 3/4″ x 7/8″, aluminum, 34-gage
(*c*) Tube-fittings, 2 pcs, 7/8″ x 1 1/2″, same
(*d*) Tube-fittings, 2 pcs, 7/8″ x 2 1/4″, same
(*h*) Tube-fittings, 2 pcs, 7/8″ x 1″, same
(*V*) Axle, 1 pc, 1/8″ diameter x 12 1/4″, dowel-rod, pine

Procedure

Fuselage

1. Cut the section, *B*, 3/16″ x 2 7/8″ in diameter, from balsa, with a coping-saw. See Plate XXI. The center of this section can best be made by laying out the opening according to the drawing, and then boring a 3/8″ hole with a sharp bit. Insert a coping-saw blade in the hole, and cut carefully to the outline. Sand the outside edge with fine sandpaper.

2. Cut the four notches, 3/32″ deep and 5/32″ wide, with a sharp chisel.

3. Sections *C, D, E,* and *F*, are all of the same thickness, and may be cut from the same piece of balsa board. Lay out the forms so that the grain of the wood runs in opposite directions in adjoining sections.

4. Cut out the sections, *C, D,* and *E*, with a coping-saw, and finish smooth with fine sandpaper. Cut the inside openings and outside notches as suggested in paragraph 1, above.

5. In making section *F*, bore a 1/4″ hole, 1/2″ from the top. This hole is to receive the rear end of the motor-stick. See cross-section drawing, Plate XXI.

6. Make the tail-piece, *G*, 1/2″ long, slanting 5/8″ to 5/16″. Cut the four notches to receive the ends of the longerons.

7. Make the four longerons, *H*, from balsa, 3/32″ x 5/32″ x 25″, finished dimensions.

Assembling the Fuselage

1. Place the four longerons, *H*, on the bench together; measure, and mark off the places where the longerons are to be fastened to the sections.

2. Fasten the four longerons *H*, to the tail-piece with ambroid. These pieces should fit in the four notches tightly. Wind

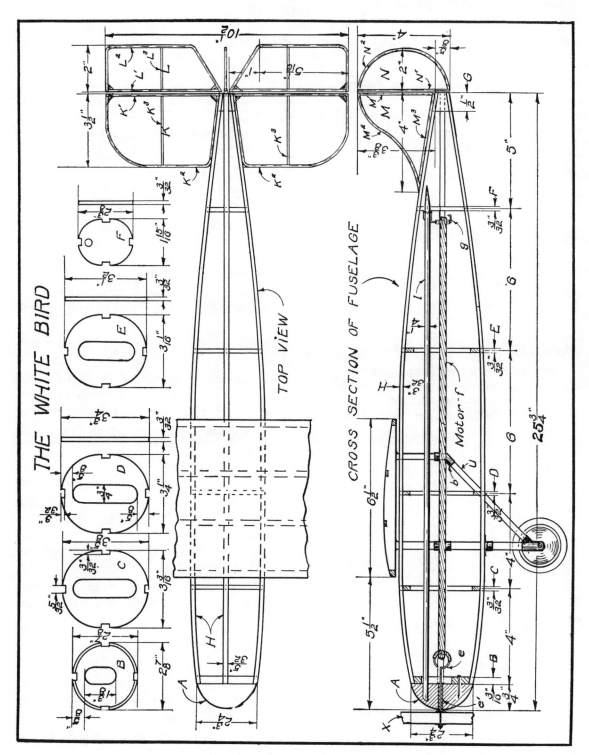

THE WHITE BIRD

TOP VIEW

CROSS SECTION OF FUSELAGE

PLATE XXI

102

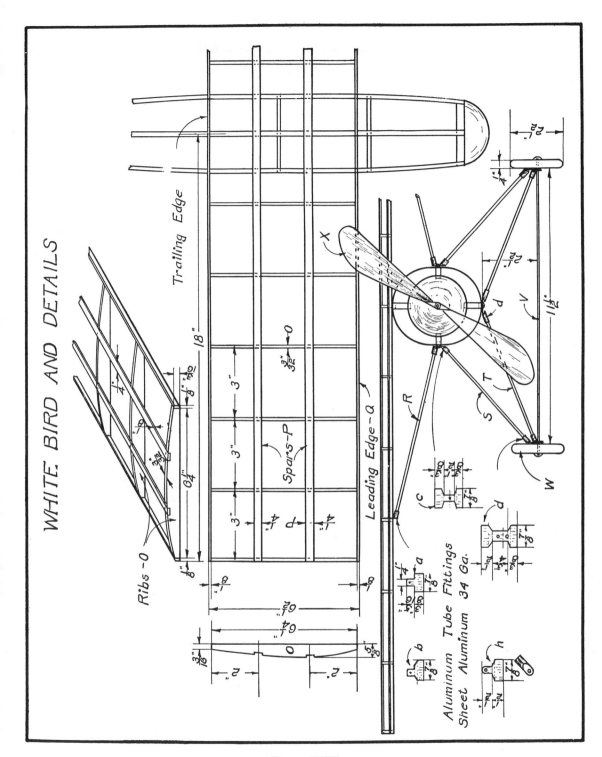

WHITE BIRD AND DETAILS

PLATE XXII

103

fine thread around the longerons at this point, to keep them in place until the ambroid is dry.

3. Ambroid the longerons to section *F*, and wind thread around the fuselage at this point, to hold the longerons tightly in place.

4. Proceed with sections *E, D, C,* and *B*, in the same manner, bending the longerons, *H,* as you attach them to the successive sections.

5. Make the nose-piece, *A*, shaping it with a sharp sloyd or pocket knife to a nice round shape. Sand it smooth with No. 4-0 sandpaper.

6. Use a $\frac{1}{4}''$ pine dowel for the motor-stick, *I*. Sharpen one end of this stick, so that it will easily fit in the $\frac{1}{4}''$ hole, section F.

7. Drill a $\frac{1}{4}''$ hole on the flat side of the nose-piece, part way into the nose, to receive the front end of the motor-stick, *I*. Fasten the motor-stick to the nose-piece with ambroid. See cross-section drawing, Plate XXI. Drill a hole through the exact center of the nose-piece to receive the bearing. The hole should be of the proper size to fit the bearing.

8. Make the rear hook, *g*, from No. .035 music-wire, and attach it through the tail end of the motor-stick. See Plate XXI.

9. We now proceed to make the other parts of the plane, such as the wing stabilizer and elevator, before completing the power-plant.

Stabilizer and Elevator

1. Make spar of the stabilizer, *K-1*, from $\frac{1}{16}'' \times \frac{1}{16}'' \times 10\frac{1}{2}''$ bamboo. Cut the edges, *K-2*, $\frac{3}{64}'' \times \frac{1}{16}'' \times 15''$, and the two ribs, *K-3*, $\frac{3}{64}'' \times \frac{1}{16}'' \times 3\frac{1}{4}''$, from bamboo also.

2. Make a full sized drawing of the stabilizer on a piece of board or drawing-paper. Build your stabilizer on top of the drawing, using small brads to hold the bent pieces in place.

3. Bend the edge of the frame, *K-2*, by steaming or warming over a candle flame. Place the bent pieces, *K-2*, on your outline, and ambroid the ends to the spar, *K-1*. Use small balsa blocks on the four corners of the stabilizer, to stiffen and strengthen it.

4. Ambroid the two ribs, *K-3*, in place.

5. Make a notch in the end of the tail-piece of the fuselage, *G*, to receive the spar of the stabilizer, *K-1*. Attach the stabilizer to the fuselage with ambroid, by inserting the cross-spar, *K-1*, in the notch of the tail. Fasten the inside edges of the stabilizer, *k-2*, to the side longerons of the fuselage with ambroid and fine silk thread.

6. Make the two spars of the elevator, *L*, from $\frac{1}{16}'' \times \frac{1}{16}'' \times 6''$ bamboo. Cut the two edges, *L-2*, $\frac{3}{64}'' \times \frac{1}{16}'' \times 10''$, and the two ribs, *L-2*, $\frac{3}{64}'' \times \frac{1}{16}'' \times 1\frac{7}{8}''$, from bamboo.

7. Follow the directions given for the stabilizer in assembling the elevator. Construct the elevator on your full-sized drawing, using brads to hold the bent edges in place. Use the small balsa corners to make the elevator more rigid.

8. Fasten the elevator to the spar of the stabilizer, *K-1*, with fine silk thread or fine wire.

Rudder and Fin

1. Make the vertical piece of the fin, *M-1*, $\frac{1}{16}'' \times \frac{1}{16}'' \times 3\frac{3}{8}''$, and the two edges, *M-2*, $\frac{3}{64}'' \times \frac{1}{16}'' \times 6''$, from bamboo.

2. Make a full-sized drawing of the fin on a piece of board. Bend the top edge by steaming or holding over a candle flame. Hold the curved edge, *M-2*, in place by using small brads, and fasten the pieces together with ambroid.

3. Fasten the fin to the top longeron of the fuselage with ambroid and fine silk thread.

4. Make the vertical piece of the rudder, N-1, $\frac{1}{16}$" x $\frac{1}{16}$" x 4", and curved edge, N-2, $\frac{3}{64}$" x $\frac{1}{16}$" x 10", from bamboo.

5. Make a full-sized drawing of the rudder on a piece of board. Bend the edge, N-2, by steaming or holding over a candle flame, and fasten it to the vertical piece, N-1, with ambroid.

6. Attach the rudder to the vertical piece, M-1, with fine silk thread or very fine wire. Rubber bands may be used to hold the rudder at a set position when flying.

The Wing

1. Cut out 13 pieces of balsa, $\frac{3}{32}$" x $\frac{5}{8}$" x $6\frac{1}{4}$", for the ribs, O. Make a full-sized pattern of one rib from heavy drawing-paper, according to the dimensions given in the drawing, Plate XXII. Trace around this pattern on one of the ribs.

2. Nail six or seven blanks together with fine brads, or pins, and cut out these ribs to the required shape with a sharp knife. Sand with fine sandpaper.

3. While these ribs are held together with fine brads, cut the two notches to receive the top spars, P.

4. In like manner, prepare the next six ribs.

5. Cut the top spars, P, to the finished dimensions, $\frac{1}{8}$" x $\frac{1}{4}$" x 36", from balsa.

6. Make the leading and trailing edges, Q, both the same size, $\frac{1}{8}$" x $\frac{3}{16}$" x 36", finished dimensions.

7. We are now ready to assemble the wing. Mark the top spars at each section where they are to be fastened to the ribs. Proceed and fasten the two top spars to each rib with a few drops of ambroid.

8. Fasten the leading and trailing edges to the ends of the 13 ribs with ambroid and a few small brads. Do not put a brad in each rib, but just enough to keep the edges intact. By winding thread around the wing, the leading and trailing edges may be held tightly in place until the ambroid is dry.

9. Round off the leading and trailing edges with fine sandpaper.

Chassis

1. Make the four wing-braces, R, $\frac{3}{32}$" x $\frac{1}{4}$" x $7\frac{1}{4}$", from balsa. Round the edges with fine sandpaper.

2. In a similar manner, construct the two chassis braces, S, $\frac{3}{32}$" x $\frac{1}{4}$" x $5\frac{1}{2}$", with the round edges.

3. Cut the two chassis braces, T, $\frac{3}{32}$" x $\frac{1}{4}$" x $5\frac{3}{4}$", and cross-braces, V, $\frac{3}{32}$" x $\frac{1}{4}$" x $7\frac{1}{2}$", from balsa. Round the edges with fine sandpaper.

4. To make the tube fittings, follow the directions given in the drawing. These fittings are made from No. 34-gage aluminum, and are very simple to make. Make the four fittings, a, first. Fasten two of these fittings to the third rib from the left end of the wing, $1\frac{1}{4}$" from the leading and trailing edges, with fine brads. In like manner fasten two fittings on the right side of the wing.

5. Make the two double fittings, c, and fasten to the side longerons with fine box-nails and ambroid.

6. Make the three fittings, d, and fasten one to the lower longeron, to receive the two braces, T. The other two fittings, d, are fitted on the axle to receive the lower ends of braces, S and T. After the fittings are bent to the proper shape, bore a $\frac{1}{8}$" hole in each to receive the axle.

7. Make two fittings, h, to fit on the lower end of each brace, U, and on the

axle. Use a ⅛″ birch dowel, 12½″ in
length, for the axle.

8. The two wheels are cut out round with
a coping-saw, and sanded to a nice finish
with fine sandpaper. The wheels may be
turned out on a lathe, if one is available.

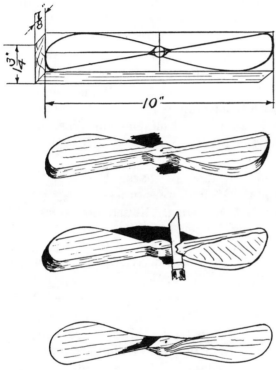

FIG. 45. Details of the propeller

Covering the Plane

1. Cover the wing, the fuselage, and the
empennage with Japanese tissue-paper.
Cover the wing on both sides, using a
heavy banana-oil for glue. Cover only a
section of the wing at a time, stretching
the paper as you proceed.

2. Cover the fuselage a section at a time
also.

3. After the entire plane is covered with
Japanese tissue paper, apply a thin coat
of dope to the paper.

Assembling the Chassis

1. Slip on the fittings, d and h, on to the
axle, as shown in the drawing, Plate XXII.
These fittings should fit the axle tightly.

2. Place the wheels on the axle, and glue
a balsa cap on each end of the axle, to
hold the wheels in place.

3. Bend the axle-fittings, d and h, around
the lower ends of the braces, S, T, and U,
tightly. In like manner, the center longeron
fittings, d, and side fittings, c, are bent
around the ends of braces, s and t. The
top fitting of brace, U, is fastened to the
side longeron with a fine box-nail.

4. Attach the wing to the fuselage, bending the fittings, a, around the ends of the
four braces, R. Use ambroid to hold these
tightly. In like manner, bend the fitting,
G, to the lower end of the front braces, R.
Fasten the lower end of the back brace, r,
to the side longerons by means of fittings, b.

Propeller

1. Make the propeller, x, from a balsa
block, ⅞″ x 1¾″ x 10″, Fig. 45. Mark the
block by drawing fine lines diagonally on
one flat surface. Make a hole at the intersection of the lines, or at the exact center
of the block, with one end of your propeller-shaft.

2. Carve the block to the diagonal lines,
leaving the center part of the block ¼″
thick, to prevent breaking while carving
the blades.

3. Draw the end diagonal lines, and
carve out the blades of the propeller, until
they taper gradually from the thickness
of the hub at the center to about 1/16″ thick
at the tips.

4. With fine sandpaper, sand each blade
so that the front is slightly rounded, and
the back part is convex.

5. Balance the propeller carefully before attaching it to the plane.

6. Give the propeller three coats of banana-oil, and sand slightly between coats.

Propeller-Shaft

1. Make the propeller-shaft from a bicycle-spoke, and use the end-nut for the bearing. Also, it is possible to purchase an ideal ball-bearing shaft-and-bearing assembly that works very nicely on this plane.

2. Insert and ambroid the bearing, *e'*, in the nose-piece of the plane, as shown in the drawing, Plate XXI.

3. Place two small brass washers on the shaft to cut down the friction between the bearing and the nose-piece.

4. Insert the shaft, *e,* in the bearing, and attach it to the propeller, as shown in the drawing. Use a small nut on the end of the shaft, to hold the propeller tightly to the shaft.

Motor

1. Use 10 strands, or about 18 feet, of $\frac{3}{16}''$ flat rubber for the motor. Attach the motor to the rear hook of the motor-stick and to the loop of the propeller-shaft.

2. We are now ready to attach the power-plant to the fuselage. For the purpose of winding the motor and for making repairs, the motor-stick and nose-piece have been made separate from the fuselage. The motor-stick with nose-piece is held to the plane by means of small hooks on both sides of the plane.

Adjusting and Flying the "White Bird"

1. To fly the "White Bird," remove the power-plant, including nose-piece, motor-stick, and rubber motor, from the plane.

2. Wind the propeller 50 to 100 times, and insert the power-plant back in the fuselage for a trial flight.

3. Set the controls in neutral, and launch the plane from your hands above your shoulders for the first trial.

4. The next trial may be made on a smooth runway, winding the motor about 100 times.

5. Keep testing your plane, until you can make it run in a straight course.

6. When you are satisfied that the plane is well adjusted, wind the motor 200 times, and try for a short flight.

7. The model can be controlled by the rudder and the elevator. It can be made to travel in a large circle by setting the rudder at an angle.

8. If the plane dives, raise the elevator; if it climbs too suddenly, lower the elevator.

9. If the plane attempts to turn over, or to go sidewise, examine it carefully, and look for a warped wing or fuselage.

Questions

1. What are the elevators of the plane for?

2. What are the ailerons?

3. Would a plane fly without a stabilizer and fin?

4. What makes aluminum so light?

CHAPTER XVII

THE "CHAMPION FLYER"

HERE, BOYS, is the most satisfactory flyer you can make, Fig. 46. It is a real champion, and will do three minutes or more. It has an official record of two minutes and fifteen seconds, made in an A.M.L.A. local contest in a small school auditorium. It has an unofficial record of three minutes and five seconds in a municipal auditorium.

The "Champion Flyer" was designed by Stanley Sonmore, while enrolled as a 9-B pupil at the Bryant Junior High School, Minneapolis. See Fig. 47. Stanley has been a model-airplane enthusiast for more than five years, beginning as a member of the Bryant Junior High School Model Airplane Club.

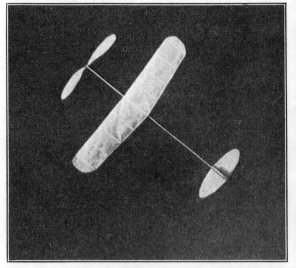

FIG. 46. The "Champion Flyer"

Materials Required

Fuselage

(A) Fuselage, 1 pc, $\frac{3}{32}$" x $\frac{5}{32}$" x $8\frac{1}{2}$", balsa

(B) Extended stick, 1 pc, $\frac{1}{32}$" x $\frac{1}{16}$" x 7", balsa

(C) Rudder, 1 pc, $\frac{1}{64}$" x $\frac{1}{32}$" x $2\frac{1}{8}$", balsa

(D) Rudder, 1 pc, $\frac{1}{64}$" x $\frac{1}{32}$" x $1\frac{1}{8}$", balsa

(E) Rudder, 1 pc, $\frac{1}{64}$" x $\frac{1}{32}$" x $1\frac{3}{4}$", balsa

(F) Elevator cross-piece, 1 pc, $\frac{1}{64}$" x $\frac{1}{32}$" x 5", balsa

(G) Elevator, 2 pcs, $\frac{1}{64}$" x $\frac{1}{32}$" x $1\frac{1}{8}$", balsa

(H) Bearing, 1 pc, $\frac{5}{16}$" x $\frac{1}{2}$" x No. 34-gage, aluminum

(h) Bearing, 1 pc, 3" long, No. .016 music-wire

(I) Rear hook, 1 pc, 3" long, No. .014 music-wire

(J) Propeller-shaft, 1 pc, 4" long, No. .014 music-wire

(K) Propeller, 1 pc, $\frac{3}{4}$" x 1" x 7", balsa

The Wing

(L) Leading edge, 1 pc, $\frac{1}{32}$" x $\frac{1}{16}$" x $12\frac{1}{2}$", balsa

(M) Trailing edge, 1 pc, $\frac{1}{32}$" x $\frac{1}{16}$" x 13", balsa

(N to O) Ribs, 9 pcs, $\frac{1}{32}$" x $\frac{1}{32}$" x $2\frac{3}{4}$", balsa

(P) Tips, 2 pcs, $\frac{1}{32}$" x $\frac{1}{32}$" x 6", balsa

(R, S) Clips, 1 pc, 7" long, No. .014 music-wire

Covering, 1 pc, 6" x 24", superfine tissue-paper

The Motor

(T) Motor, 1 pc, $\frac{3}{64}$" x $\frac{3}{64}$" square x 18" long, rubber band

(*U*) Bead washer, 1 pc
Landing-gear, optional, 1 pc, 12" long, No. .014 music-wire

Procedure

Fuselage

1. Cut a piece of balsa, 1/8" x 3/16" x 8½", for the fuselage, *A*, and sand it to the finished dimensions, 3/32" x 5/32" x 8½", with No. 4-0 sandpaper. Then cut and sand the fuselage so that it is 5/32" in width at the center, slanting to 3/32" on each end. See detail drawing, Plate XXIII. Make sure that your stick is not thicker or wider than the dimensions given. Remember, the lighter the plane, the longer the flight.

2. With a razor-blade, put a groove at the rear end of the motor-stick, *A*, to receive the extended tail-piece, *B*.

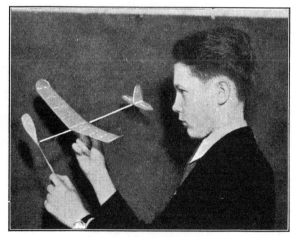

FIG. 47. The "Champion Flyer" and its Designer

Bearing

1. Make the bearing, *H*, from a piece of No. 34-gage aluminum, or bearing, *h*, from a piece of No. .016 music-wire, or, a small brad flattened with a hammer will do very nicely also. See details in Plate XXIII.

2. If you choose the aluminum or brad bearing, drill a hole through the metal with a No. 70 drill or a phonograph-needle. Bend the bearing to the shape shown in the drawing. The designer of the original model, Stanley Sonmore, used an aluminum bearing on his "Champion Flyer."

3. The wire bearing, made from No. .016 music-wire, is probably the easiest bearing to make. Make a small loop on one end of the wire by bending around a fine brad or a needle. Use small round-nose pliers for the job.

4. Ambroid or cement the bearing, *H*, to the lower front end of your motor-stick. Make sure that the ambroid or cement is dry before proceeding with the next step.

Rear Hook

1. Bend the rear hook, *I*, from a piece of No. .016 music-wire, to the shape shown in the drawing. Shape this wire hook with round-nose pliers, and cement to the lower rear end of the motor-stick, *A*, Plate XXIII. The center of the loop of the rear hook should be about 5/32" from the motor-stick, and in line with the hole in the bearing, *H*.

Extended Elevator

1. Cut the extended stick, *B*, 1/32" x 1/16" x 7", from balsa, and shape it to 1/16" in width on one end slanting to 1/32" on the elevator end.

2. Make the cross-piece, *F*, 1/64" x 1/32" x 5", from balsa. Ambroid or cement this piece to the extended stick, *B*, 7/8" from the end.

3. Make the two end-pieces, *G*, 1/64" x 1/32" x 1⅛", from balsa, and ambroid these pieces to the long cross-piece, *F*, as shown in the drawing, Plate XXIII.

4. Cover the elevator with fine Japanese tissue-paper.

5. Paint the under part of the elevator

THE CHAMPION FLYER
R.O.G. Model Plane

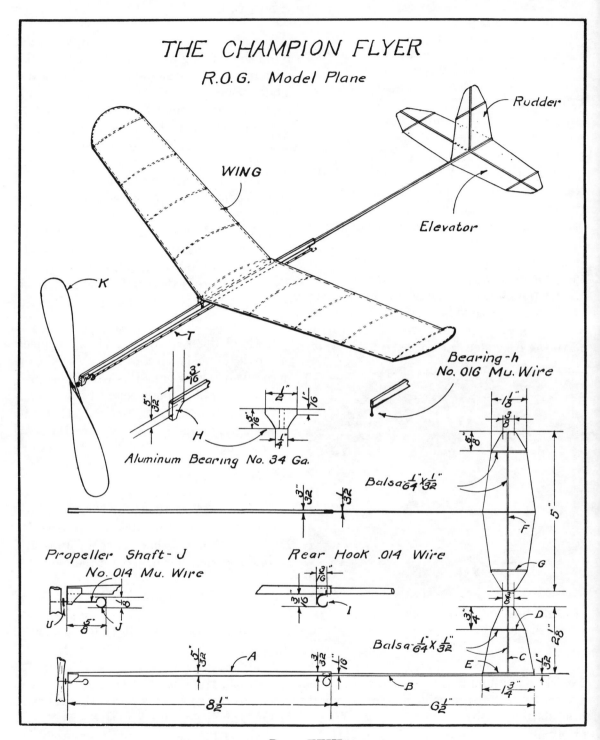

Rudder

WING

Elevator

K

T

Bearing-h
No. 016 Mu. Wire

$\frac{3}{16}$"

$\frac{5}{32}$"

H

2"

$\frac{1}{16}$"

$\frac{5}{16}$"

$\frac{1}{4}$"

Aluminum Bearing No. 34 Ga.

Balsa $\frac{1}{64}$"× $\frac{1}{32}$"

$\frac{1}{8}$"

$\frac{3}{8}$"

$\frac{5}{8}$"

F

G

5"

Propeller Shaft-J
No. 014 Mu. Wire

$\frac{1}{8}$"

U

$\frac{5}{8}$"

J

Rear Hook .014 Wire

$\frac{3}{16}$"

$\frac{3}{16}$"

I

$\frac{3}{8}$"

$\frac{3}{4}$"

D

Balsa $\frac{1}{64}$"× $\frac{1}{32}$"

E

C

$2\frac{1}{8}$"

$\frac{1}{32}$"

$\frac{5}{32}$"

A

$\frac{3}{32}$"

$\frac{1}{16}$"

O

B

$8\frac{1}{2}$"

$6\frac{1}{2}$"

$1\frac{3}{4}$"

$\frac{3}{32}$"

$\frac{3}{32}$"

PLATE XXIII

THE CHAMPION FLYER
Wing and Propeller Details

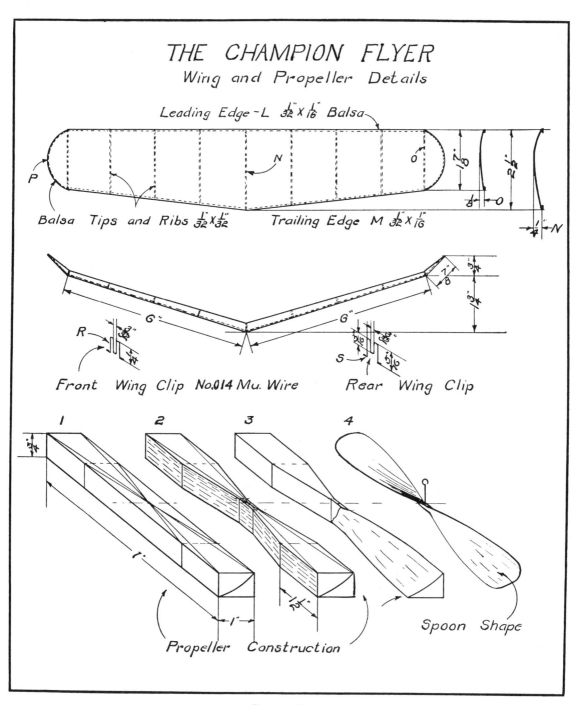

Leading Edge – L $\frac{1}{32}" \times \frac{1}{16}"$ Balsa

Balsa Tips and Ribs $\frac{1}{32}" \times \frac{1}{32}"$ Trailing Edge M $\frac{1}{32}" \times \frac{1}{16}"$

Front Wing Clip No.014 Mu. Wire   Rear Wing Clip

Propeller Construction   Spoon Shape

PLATE XXIV

111

with thick banana-oil, and attach the tissue-paper.

Rudder

1. Make the rudder from the following balsa pieces: one vertical piece, *C*, $\frac{1}{64}''$ x $\frac{1}{32}''$ x $2\frac{1}{8}''$; one cross-piece, *D*, $\frac{1}{64}''$ x $\frac{1}{32}''$ x $1\frac{1}{8}''$; and one base piece, *E*, $\frac{1}{64}''$ x $\frac{1}{32}''$ x $1\frac{3}{4}''$. Assemble the rudder with ambroid to the shape shown in the drawing, Plate XXIII.

2. Attach the fine Japanese paper to one side of the rudder, using banana-oil.

3. Attach the rudder to the top and rear end of the extended stick with ambroid. Use very little ambroid, but work fast when applying.

4. Dip the big end of the extended stick, *B*, in ambroid or cement, and attach it to the motor-stick, placing it in the opening. This extended tail may be attached at a small angle or curve, so as to cause the plane to fly in a circle.

The Wing

1. A wing of the cambered type illustrated in the "Champion Flyer" requires patience and accurate workmanship on the part of the builder. See Plate XXIV. It is advisable to use a wing form to hold spars, ribs, and tips in place, and to insure the proper angle in the wing. The form can be used not only as a bending device, but also as a wing holder when the plane is not in use.

2. Make the form according to the drawing, Fig. 48, from a block of wood or some heavy cardboard. The angle or V-shaped block represents the dihedral angle of the wing. The purpose of the dihedral angle or V-shaped wing is to give the plane stability; or, in other words, to keep the plane steady while flying.

3. Draw the outline of the wing on the form with a heavy pencil, including all balsa parts, such as the leading edge, trailing edge, tips, and ribs.

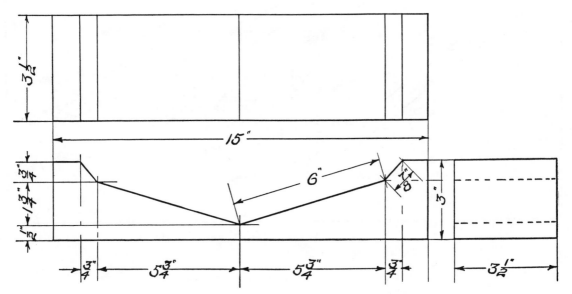

FIG. 48. Details of wing-form for the "Champion Flyer"

The Spars

1. Make the leading edge, L, $\frac{1}{32}$" x $\frac{1}{16}$" x 12", and the trailing edge, M, $\frac{1}{32}$" x $\frac{1}{16}$" x 12$\frac{1}{2}$", from balsa. Make sure that these spars are sanded down to the proper thicknesses and widths. Use No. 4-0 sandpaper.

2. Bend the two spars, leading edge, L, and trailing edge, M, at the center. If the balsa is brittle, use hot water or steam to soften before bending.

3. Place the bent spars in the form, on the outline, and nail four or five wooden cleats across the spars, with small brads, to hold them in place. When nailing cleats, make sure that you barely touch the balsa spars. The spars may also be held in place with pins.

The Ribs

1. Make all ribs from balsa, $\frac{1}{32}$" x $\frac{1}{32}$". Make the center rib, N, first, according to the shape shown in the detail drawings, Plate XXIV. It should be 2$\frac{1}{2}$" in length after it is bent, and should have a camber of $\frac{1}{4}$" at the center.

2. The ribs may be softened by steaming or boiling in water, before bending around a form of the desired shape. They may also be bent dry by crushing the balsa into the required curve.

3. After the center rib is ambroided or cemented in place, proceed to make the two end ribs, N.

4. The ribs betwen the center and the end ribs are of different lengths and heights, according to the slanted shape of the wing.

The Clips

1. Make the front wing-clip, R, and the rear wing-clip, S, from No. .014 music-wire. Bend the clips according to the detail drawing, Plate XXIV, with round-nose pliers. Be sure that the center opening of each clip is bent to fit the fuselage tightly.

2. The difference between the heights of the front and the rear clip gives the wing an upward slant, to make the plane climb. This upward slant is called the *angle of incidence,* and should be checked very carefully.

3. When the clips are of the proper shape, cement one exactly in the center of each spar, underneath.

Covering the Wing

1. Experience shows that a single-surface wing should be covered on the upper side of the frame. The upper surface of an airplane wing gives the greatest amount of lift. Use superfine tissue-paper to cover the wing. This is probably the best light paper now in use for covering model planes for endurance flights. It is best to cover each half of the wing with a separate piece of paper. Place the tissue-paper between sheets of newspaper, and press with a hot iron before attaching it to the wing.

2. Paint the leading edge, L, of one-half of the wing with banana-oil, and attach the paper to the edge. Then, paint the trailing edge, M, with banana-oil, and set the paper back over the wing, attaching it to the trailing edge. Do not pull the paper too tightly between the ribs.

3. Paint with banana-oil directly over each rib on top of the paper with a very fine brush. Paint the top of the wing tip, pulling the paper over in place.

4. When dry, trim the edges of the tissue-paper off with a razor-blade.

5. In like manner, cover the second half of the wing.

Propeller

1. Success in making an endurance flying model depends to a great extent on the propeller. The propeller by revolving at

a moderate rate of speed pulls the model craft through the air. Follow the detail drawing, Plate XXIV, in making the propeller for your "Champion Flyer."

2. Cut out a block, ¾" x 1" x 7", from a good soft straight-grained piece of balsa. Lay out the propeller by drawing lines from corner to corner diagonally on one surface, Step 1. Make a small hole at the intersection of the lines, and at the exact center of the block, with a pin.

3. Draw a second set of diagonal lines 1½" from the ends, as shown in Step 2.

4. Carve the block to these diagonal lines, leaving the center section about ⅛" in thickness, Step 2. This part is left thicker to prevent the block from breaking while carving the blades.

5. Draw the end diagonal lines next, which show the end shape and pitch of your propeller. They should run in opposite directions. See Steps 2 and 3.

6. Carve out the blades of the propeller carefully, until they are about 1/16" thick, and spoon shaped, Step 4.

7. Finish the propeller with No. 4-0 sandpaper. When complete, the blades should not be over 1/32" in thickness, and the hub not more than 1/16" thick. Follow the directions carefully in carving out your propeller.

Propeller-Shaft

1. Make the propeller-shaft, *J*, from No. .014 music-wire. Make a ⅛" loop on one end of the shaft, and insert the shaft in the propeller, as shown in the drawing, Plate XXIII.

2. Make a small U-bend in the wire, and ambroid securely to the propeller.

3. Place one small bead on the shaft, to cut down the friction between the bearing and the propeller.

The Motor

1. The power on the "Champion Flyer" is obtained from a piece of para rubber band, 3/64" x 3/64" square x 18" long, or two strands of rubber tied in a square knot. There should be about ¾" slack when the motor is attached to the fuselage.

2. Good para rubber can be stretched about nine times its length when released. Do not leave the motor wound when the plane is not in use, or the rubber will stretch and lose its strength.

3. Using a lubricant on your motor, such as glycerin, makes it possible to give the rubber more turns, and insures a more even flow of power.

Landing-Gear

1. Although the drawing of the "Champion Flyer" shows no landing-gear, one may be added by using No. .014 music-wire, to suit the builder's plans.

Adjusting and Flying the "Champion Flyer"

1. Attach the wing to the fuselage at a point close to the elevator.

2. After you have assembled your plane, allow it to glide from your hand, to test its balance.

3. Wind the motor with propeller, about 25 to 50 turns, and make necessary adjustments.

4. If the plane tries to climb too rapidly, set the wing back. If it dives quickly, set the wing forward a little, and try again. When you have experimented, and are satisfied that your "Champion Flyer" glides nicely and evenly, wind the motor 300 to 500 times for a trial flight.

5. Since the "Champion Flyer" is an

indoor model plane, you will want the plane to fly in a circle, the size of the circle path depending on the size of the room, auditorium, or hall.

6. By curving the rudder to the left, for example, on a right-handed propeller, the plane can be adjusted to follow a circular path. Or the rudder may be attached to the extended stick with a slight curve in it, when the plane is assembled.

Questions

1. What is meant by the angle of incidence?

2. What is meant by the dihedral angle in an airplane?

3. What effect will a spoon-shaped propeller have on an endurance record?

4. What is meant by the torque effect?

5. What is meant by the washout in the wing of a model airplane?

CHAPTER XVIII

A TAILLESS KITE

HERE, BOYS, is the easiest kite that you can make, and it is always sure to fly. Of the several thousands of kites made on our playgrounds each year, the 36″ Tailless Kite is the most popular, and the best flyer of them all. This same Malay two-stick kite is the first one to appear in the air in the early spring of the year, and the last to fly its colors in the fall.

The features of this kite are that it is easy to make, it flies easily in a very light breeze, and it can always be depended on to be a steady as well as a high flyer.

There is nothing new about this kite. It is said that the people of the Malay Peninsula have used this type of kite for many centuries.

Tailless Kite

Materials Required

(A) Spine, 1 pc, ¼″ x 5⁄16″ x 36″, pine or bass
(B) Bow, 1 pc, ¼″ x 5⁄16″ x 36″, same
(C) Brace, 1 pc, ¼″ x ¼″ x 3½″, same
(D) Kite-string and line, cotton twine, 7-ply
(E) Covering, tissue-paper, or crêpe-paper

Procedure

Framework

1. Cut the spine, A and bow-stick, B, from bass or pine, ¼″ x 5⁄16″ x 36″. See Plate XXV. Saw in or notch the ends of both sticks and reinforce these ends with fine thread, as shown in the drawing.

2. The bow-stick, B, is placed from ¼ to ⅕ the distance down from the top of the spine. In this case it is 9″ from the top.

3. It is best to lash the spine and the bow sticks together instead of nailing them. A nail or even a small brad will weaken the bow-stick. Be sure to find the exact center of the bow-stick, before lashing the sticks together.

Stringing the Kite

1. Bend the bow-stick back, and string it with 5-ply or 7-ply cotton string. The ¼″ x ¼″ x 3¼″ brace is used to get the proper bend in the bow. This brace can be removed after the kite is complete.

2. Pass a piece of 5-ply or 7-ply cotton twine around the entire frame in notches, and fasten the string at one point.

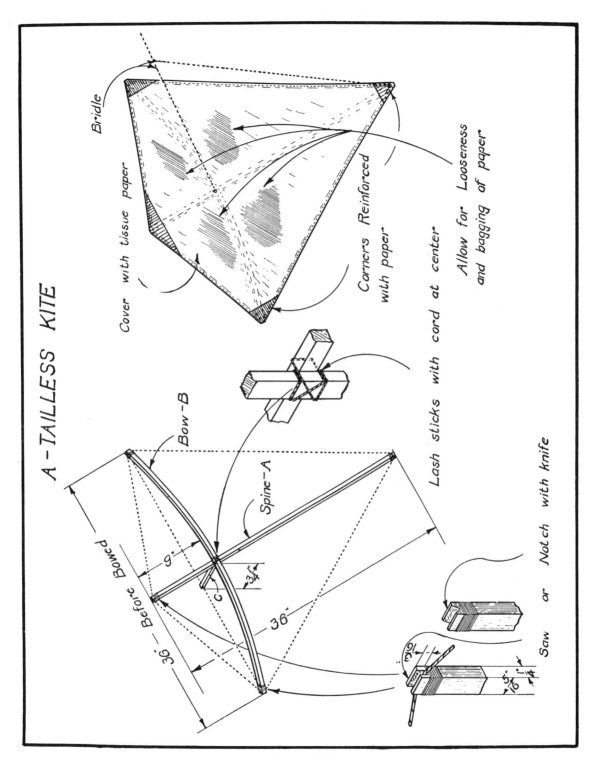

A-TAILLESS KITE

Bridle

Cover with tissue paper

Corners Reinforced with paper

Allow for Looseness and bagging of paper

Lash sticks with cord at center

Bow-B

Spine-A

9"

3/4"

c

36"

36" — Before Bowed

36"

Saw or Notch with knife

PLATE XXV

117

3. The adjustment between points or sticks is best made after the frame is strung. Shift the upper or lower parts of the kite until the left and right sides are exactly alike. Make sure that your kite is well balanced and symmetrical.

The Covering

1. Tissue-paper is used in covering kites more than any other kind of covering material. Tissue-paper may be obtained in all shades and tints of colors to suit one's taste. Crêpe-paper may also be used with good results.

2. Lay your paper on the floor or a table. Place your kite frame on the paper, and mark around the string of the frame. Then cut the paper 1½" outside of the mark, or 1½" larger than the frame, on all sides.

3. A tailless kite requires a loose and bagging covering. Instead of folding in the entire 1½" margin, turn only ¾" on the outer edge. This will leave plenty of looseness and bagging of the paper.

4. Fasten the edges down with paste.

The Bridle

1. A kite is not complete until the bridle (or belly band) is attached. A kite depends on its bridle for the right distribution of pull by the line. The angle of the kite exposed to the breeze also depends on the bridle.

2. On this kite the bridle may be attached at the bottom of the spine and at the crossing of the bow and spine.

3. The bridle must be long enough so that when it is drawn over the side of the kite, the loop will reach the outer point of the bow, as shown in the drawing.

The Kite-Line

1. A 5-ply to 7-ply cotton twine is very satisfactory for a kite of this size. Even the lighter cotton wrapping string will prove quite satisfactory.

2. See Chapter XXIII, The Minneapolis City-Wide Kite Tournament.

Questions

1. What does a lack of balance mean?
2. Why should you allow for looseness and bagging of the kite covering?
3. Which is best adhesive to use, paste or glue?
4. It is said that the bridle is a very important part of a kite. Why?

CHAPTER XIX

A FRENCH WAR-KITE

NEXT TO THE 36″ Tailless Kite, the French War-Kite is probably the best type of a kite you can make. This kite is sometimes described as a triangular box-kite with wings, and is indeed a very popular kite with the boys and girls here in Minneapolis. There are a great many of these kites entered in our city-wide tournaments, conducted by the Recreation Department of the Park Board each Summer. The French War-Kite is always steady in the air, and is a very strong puller.

Materials Required

(*A, B*) Covering, tissue-paper, cambric, or silk
(*C*) Spine, 2 pcs, ¼″ x ⁵⁄₁₆″ x 36″, pine or bass
(*D*) Bow, 1 pc, ¼″ x ⁵⁄₁₆″ x 36″, same
(*E*) Keel-stick, 1 pc, ¼″ x ⁵⁄₁₆″ x 36″, same
Kite-string and line, cotton twine, 5-ply or 7-ply

Procedure

1. Cut the four sticks, ¼″ x ⁵⁄₁₆″ x 36″, from bass, pine, or butternut, or some similar soft wood. See Plate XXVI.

2. Saw in or notch the ends of the spine, *C*, and the bow, *D*.

3. Reinforce the ends of each stick with fine thread, as shown in the drawing. The thread around the sticks is used to prevent the ends from splitting.

4. The two spines, *C*, are lashed to the horizontal bow, *C*, with fine cotton string or thread. Place the spines 12″ apart, and

French War-Kite

the bow 12″ from the top of the spines, as shown in the drawings.

5. After the kite has been strung and covered, the lashing of the spines and bow may be cut and removed, in order to roll up the kite when not in use.

The Keel

1. Make and attach the keels, *B*, before covering the wings.

2. Use tissue-paper or cambric cloth in covering the keels, *B*, and the wings, *A*. Silk is probably the best covering material for a kite of this type, but very few boys seem willing to use it. Although a kite covered with tissue-paper will fly in a lighter breeze, a kite covered with cloth is more durable.

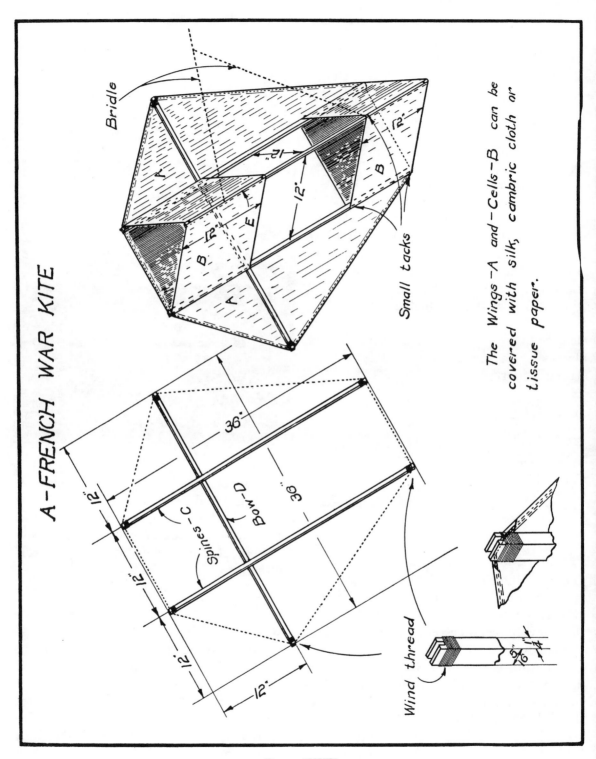

A-FRENCH WAR KITE

Bridle

12"
12"
12"
B
B
E
A
Small tacks

The Wings -A and -Cells -B can be covered with silk, cambric cloth or tissue paper.

36"
36"
12"
12"
12"
12"
12"
Spines - C
Bow - D
Wind thread

PLATE XXVI

3. Cut two pieces of cloth, 12¼″ x 36¼″, for the keels, *B*, and hem the edges. Pass the cloth around the ends of the spines, as shown, and sew the ends together.

4. Tack the cloth with very fine tacks to the spines, *C*, and to keel-stick, *E*, thus forming the triangular keels, *B*.

Covering the Wings

1. Cut two pieces of cloth to cover the wings, allowing for a ⅜″ seam to go around the string.

2. Tack the straight edge of each wing piece to the spines with fine tacks underneath the kite. Fold the outside edges around the string, and sew the hem, as shown in the drawing.

3. By removing the bow-stick, *D*, the kite can be rolled up when not in use.

Bridle and Kite-Line

1. Use a 7-ply cotton twine for the bridle and the kite-line.

2. The bridle on a kite of this type can be very easily adjusted, and there is no trick in flying the French War-Kite. Attach one end of the bridle, 7″ from the top of the kite, to the keel-stick, *E*, and the other end 12″ from the bottom of stick, *E*, as shown in drawing, Plate XXVI.

3. A 7-ply cotton twine is usually strong enough to fly this kite, but you may use seine-cord or some other kite-line of your own, if you prefer.

4. See Chapter XXIII, The Minneapolis City-Wide Kite Tournament.

Questions

1. Why should you not use fine wire for the lashings on your kite?

2. What features or characteristics make this type of kite a very good flyer?

3. Why is this called a French War-Kite?

4. Why is cloth better suited than paper for the covering on a kite of this type?

CHAPTER XX

A BOX-KITE

YOU MAY have to use a bit more skill and care in making this kite, but a little extra time and care are well worth while, when the result is a beautiful kite that will fly to the clouds when completed. It is true that a box-kite of this type requires a fairly strong breeze to keep it up in the air, but this rectangular box-kite is a real flyer, and is sure to give you endless pleasure in flying it. Lawrence Hargrave, an Australian, is given the credit for having invented the box-kite in New South Wales, in the year 1892. We read, however, that the Chinese and Japanese were flying some similar kites centuries ago.

Rectangular box-kites of this type have been used extensively by scientists for experimental purposes.

Materials Required

(*A*) Main sticks, 4 pcs, ¼″ x ½″ x 48″, pine, bass, or spruce

(*B*) Cross-braces, 8 pcs, ¼″ x ⅝″ x 24½″, same

(*C*) String-braces, light fish-line, or seine-cord

(*D*) Kite-line and bridle, seine-cord, medium-laid

Box-Kite

Procedure

1. Cut the four main sticks, *A*, ¼″ x 1½″ x 48″, from bass, pine, butternut, or spruce. See Plate XXVII.

2. Cut the eight cross-braces, *B*, ¼″ x ⅝″ x 24½″, from the same kind of wood.

3. Make each end of each brace, *B*, fork-shaped, as shown in the drawing. This can be done with a saw and ¼″ chisel.

4. Reinforce these ends with fine thread or cotton string.

5. The center portion of each brace, *B*, is to be reduced in size, to ¼″ x ¼″ square, or made round. These sticks should be as light as possible.

6. Draw the rectangular shape of one end of the kite on a piece of paper, full size, 12″ x 22″, in order to obtain an accurate measurement of the length of the diagonal braces, *B*,

Stringing the Kite

1. Make a small notch on each main stick, *A*, at the point where the string is to be fastened to the kite.

2. It is difficult to string a box-kite without some device to hold the kite square during the process. The following suggestion usually works very well. Take two pieces of cardboard, pressboard, or wood, 12″ x 12″, and cut a notch in each corner to receive the sticks, *A*. These end-boards will hold your kite square and firm, while you attach the string and cover.

3. Insert the braces, *B*, in their proper places in the kite next. Four braces may be used, but eight braces will hold up the shape of the kite much better. The eight braces, *B*, must be very light.

4. String the kite, making a loop or a knot around each main stick, at the points shown in the drawing. Use a light fish-line for these four main strings.

5. Attach the string cross-braces, *C*, using a light fish-line. If the fish-line can not be obtained, the common cotton string will do, but it is not as durable and strong as fish-line.

Covering the Kite

1. Cover the kite with tissue-paper, crêpe-paper, or cloth. For pleasure flying, I suggest that the kite be covered with paper, either tissue or crêpe. Use two different shades of paper, such as your school colors.

2. Cover the main cells with paper of one color, and the diamonds or designs with paper of another color. Make sure that the paper is put on as tightly as possible, using paste for fastening the ends together. The paper should be doubled or hemmed on the edges or on both ends of the cells.

3. If you are looking for an endurance record, or wish to use your kite for scientific purposes, use silk or cambric cloth for the covering.

BOX KITE

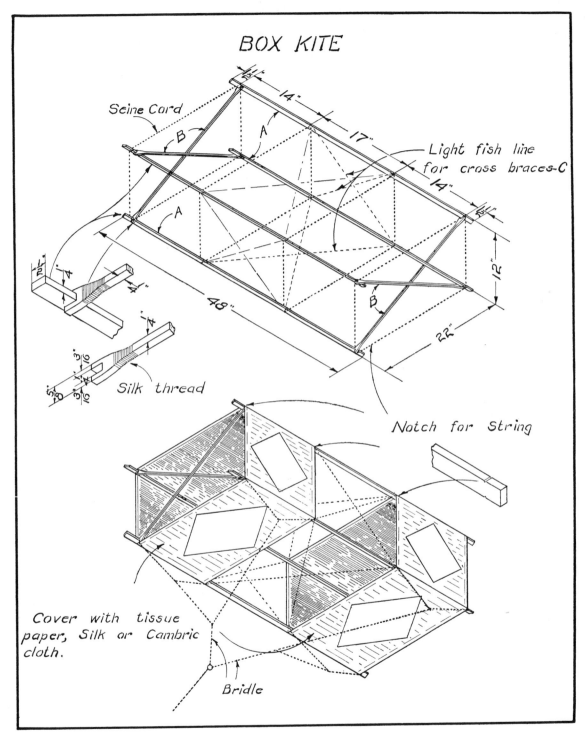

Seine Cord

B

A

14"

17"

A

Light fish line
for cross braces-C

14"

12"

48"

22"

Silk thread

Notch for String

Cover with tissue
paper, Silk or Cambric
cloth.

Bridle

PLATE XXVII

123

Bridle and Kite-Line

1. Use a medium-laid seine-cord for the bridle and the kite-line. If this type of cord is not obtainable in your district, use a 7-ply to 10-ply cotton twine.

2. Attach the bridle to the kite, as shown in the drawing. Make sure that each side of the bridle is properly balanced, and that the strings are of the proper lengths. Experiment with the bridle, until you discover the best arrangement of the bridle for the best flying of your kite.

3. Attach the kite-line to the bridle, and your kite is ready for a trip to the clouds.

4. See Chapter XXIII, The Minneapolis City-Wide Kite Tournament.

Questions

1. What kinds of scientific experiments can be made with a kite?

2. Was Benjamin Franklin's experiment with a kite a very safe one?

Chapter XXI

A BOX-KITE WITH WINGS

Box-Kite with Wings

W E HAVE on our playgrounds and in our school shops each year a number of ambitious boys who like to make the larger and more difficult kites. For these ambitious boys, I know of no better project than the large box-kite with wings, illustrated in Plate XXVIII. A kite of this type has a very strong lifting power, and is an excellent flyer in a strong wind.

Materials Required

(A) Main sticks, 4 pcs, $\frac{5}{16}''$ x $\frac{7}{16}''$ x 50'', pine, bass, or spruce
(B) Cross-braces, 4 pcs, $\frac{1}{4}''$ x $\frac{5}{8}''$ x 31'', same
(C) Wing-stick, 1 pc, $\frac{5}{16}''$ x $\frac{7}{16}''$ x 63'', same
(D, E) Covering, 1 pc, 36'' wide x 4½ yds. long, cambric or paper
Kite-line and bridle, seine-cord, medium-laid

Procedure

1. Proceed by making a regular square box-kite first, and then add the wings, D, after the square kite is completed. See Plate XXVIII. Cut the four main sticks, A, $\frac{5}{16}''$ x $\frac{7}{16}''$ x 50'', from pine, bass, or spruce.

2. Cut the brace, B, $\frac{1}{4}''$ x $\frac{5}{8}''$ x 31'', and wing-stick, C, $\frac{5}{16}''$ x $\frac{7}{16}''$ x 63'', from the same kind of wood as main sticks.

3. To insure accurate measurement of the length of the braces, B, make a full-sized lay-out of one end of the kite on a piece of wrapping-paper.

4. Make each end of each brace, B, fork-shaped, as shown in the drawing. Use a back-saw and ¼'' chisel to accomplish this job.

5. The center portion of each brace, B, is then reduced in size, to $\frac{5}{16}''$ x $\frac{3}{8}''$.

6. Reinforce the forks of the braces, B, and wing-stick, C, with fine thread.

Stringing the Kite

1. A kite of this type may be covered with either medium-weight wrapping-paper or cloth. If you decide to use paper, it is best to string the kite as shown in the drawing. In either case, however, the stringing of the kite is desirable.

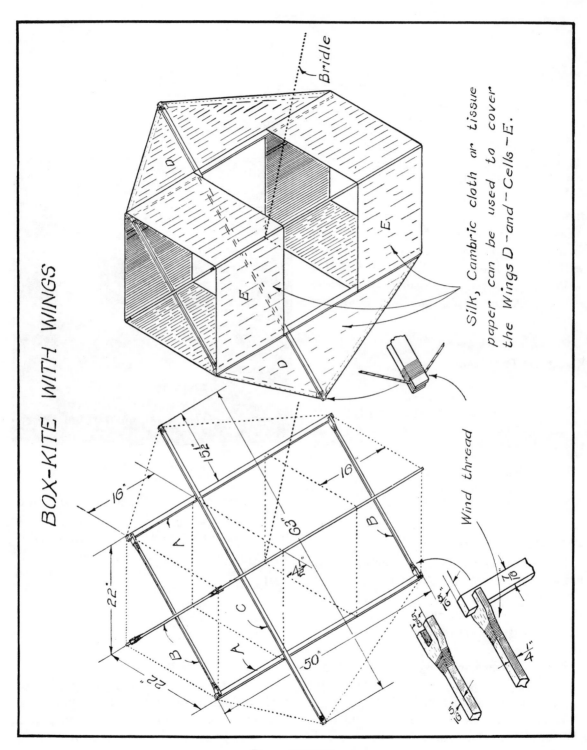

BOX-KITE WITH WINGS

Bridle

Silk, Cambric cloth or tissue
paper can be used to cover
the Wings D-and-Cells-E.

Wind thread

PLATE XXVIII

126

2. Make a small notch on each main stick, *A*, at the points where the string is to be fastened to the kite.

3. Insert the braces, *B*, in their places between the main sticks, *A*.

4. String the kite next, making a loop or a knot around each main stick at the points shown in the drawing. Use a light fish-line for stringing the four main cells.

Covering the Kite

1. Cover the kite with medium-weight wrapping-paper or cambric cloth. I prefer the cloth to the paper. A kite of this type covered with cloth is more lasting and probably performs better than the kite covered with paper.

2. Cut two pieces of cambric cloth, 16½″ x 88½″, allow ¼″ hem on the edges, and sew the ends of each piece together forming the box-cells, *E*. Make the cells, *E*, a bit smaller than 22″ square, allowing for the stretching of the cloth.

3. Tack the cloth to the main sticks, *A*, with No. 1½ tacks.

4. String the wings, *D*, next, and insert the wing-stick, *C*, in its proper place.

5. Cut two pieces of cloth for the wings, to the size shown in the drawing, allowing for a ¼″ hem on two sides.

6. Tack the straight edge of each wing-piece to the sticks, *A*, with fine tacks underneath the kite. Fold the outside edges around the wing string, and sew the hem.

7. By removing the wing-stick, *C*, and the four cross-braces, *B*, the wing can be folded when not in use.

Bridle and Kite-Line

1. Use a medium-laid seine-cord for the bridle and the kite-line. A heavy cotton twine also works very satisfactorily on this kite.

2. The bridle of this kite is an extension of the kite-line. Attach the kite-line to the outside center main stick, 11½″ from the top of the kite, or 4½″ from the lower edge of the top cell, *E*.

3. See Chapter XXIII, The Minneapolis City-Wide Kite Tournament.

Questions

1. Why does a large kite require a stronger breeze than a smaller one?

2. What makes the direction and velocity of the wind at the surface of the earth so deceptive?

3. What conclusions may you draw from observing the smoke pouring from the tops of tall chimneys with respect to the breezes that may affect the flying of your kite?

4. What dangers are involved in flying a kite out in the city streets?

Chapter XXII

A NOVELTY KITE

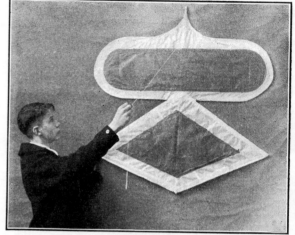

Novelty Kite

EVERY summer during our playground season, a number of Novelty Kites make their appearance as a part of the display of thousands of kites constructed by the boys and girls. The kite illustrated in Plate XXIX stood out conspicuously as a very fine flyer at one of our City-Wide Kite Tournaments, here in Minneapolis. A number of these kites of various designs were made and flown by Chinese boys. The framework of this type of kite is constructed entirely from bamboo.

Materials Required

(*A*) Spine, 1 pc, $\frac{3}{8}$″ x $\frac{1}{2}$″ x 40″, bamboo.
(*B*) Wing-spars, 2 pcs, $\frac{1}{4}$″ x $\frac{3}{8}$″ x 50″, same
(*C*) Cross-stick, 1 pc, $\frac{1}{4}$″ x $\frac{3}{8}$″ x 40″, same
(*D*) Braces, 2 pcs, $\frac{1}{4}$″ x $\frac{1}{4}$″ x 26″, same
(*E*) Braces, 2 pcs, $\frac{1}{8}$″ x $\frac{1}{4}$″ x 18″, same

Procedure

Framework

1. The pieces for the frame-work may be cut from a good-sized bamboo fish-pole.

2. Cut the spine, *A*, $\frac{3}{8}$″ x $\frac{1}{2}$″ x 40″. This piece should be the strongest part of your kite. See Plate XXIX.

3. Cut the wing-spars, *B*, $\frac{1}{4}$″ x $\frac{3}{8}$″ x 50″. These two pieces should be gradually tapered to the ends, as shown in the drawing.

4. Splice the ends of the spars together with glue and fine thread, to the shape shown in the drawing.

5. Lash the wing to the spine with fine thread or cotton string. Make sure that you locate the exact center of each spar before attaching to the spine.

6. Cut the braces, *E*, $\frac{1}{8}$″ x $\frac{1}{4}$″, and plane to about $\frac{3}{16}$″ in thickness. Attach these braces to the spine and to the top of the wing with strong thread. These braces help to keep the wing straight and balanced.

7. Cut the cross-stick, *C*, $\frac{1}{4}$″ x $\frac{3}{8}$″, and lash it to the spine. This cross-piece should be attached at a point 8″ from the bottom of the spine.

8. Cut the braces, *D*, $\frac{1}{4}$″ x $\frac{1}{4}$″ x 26″, and bend the ends, as shown in the drawing. Lash the braces, *D*, to the spine, *A*, to the lower part of the wing, *B*, and to the ends of the cross-sticks, *C*. Use fine thread and glue in lashing the pieces together.

9. String the lower part of the kite with cotton twine or light fish-line.

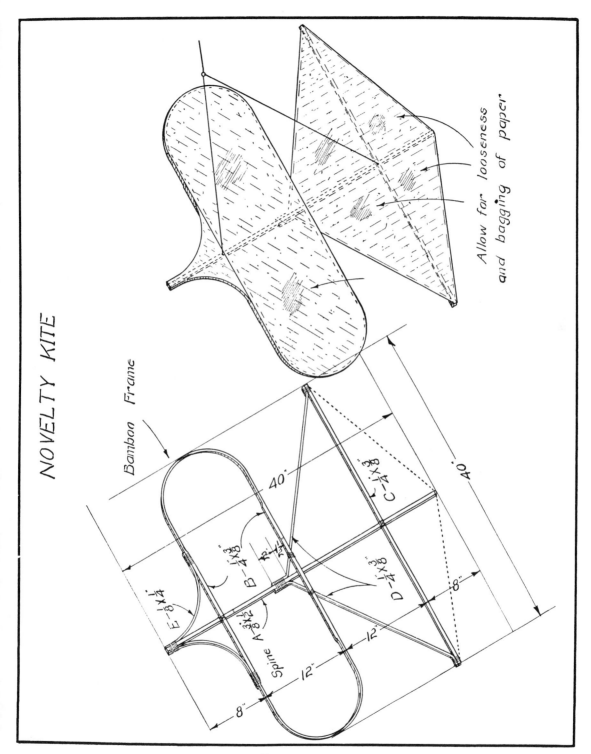

NOVELTY KITE

Allow for looseness and bagging of paper

Bamboo Frame

Spine A $\frac{3}{8} \times 1\frac{1}{2}$"

B $-\frac{1}{4} \times \frac{3}{8}$"

C $-\frac{1}{4} \times \frac{3}{8}$"

D $-\frac{1}{4} \times \frac{3}{8}$"

E $-\frac{1}{8} \times 1\frac{1}{4}$"

R $-2\frac{1}{2}$"

40"

40"

8"

8"

12"

12"

8"

PLATE XXIX

129

Covering the Kite

1. Cover the entire kite with rice-paper or crêpe-paper, using paste or cement. Lay the paper on the floor, or on a table. Place the kite-frame on the paper, and mark around the framework.

2. Cut the paper 2″ outside the mark, or 2″ larger than the frame on all sides. This type of kite requires a fairly loose and bagging covering. Instead of folding down the entire 2″ margin, turn about ¾″ of the outer edge, and glue the edges down.

Bridle and Kite-Line

1. Use a 5-ply to 7-ply cotton twine for the bridle and the kite-line. A light fish-line may be used, if preferred.

2. The bridle may be attached to the top of the wing, and at the cross-brace, C. A bit of experimenting will be necessary before you locate the exact points at which to fasten the bridle to the kite.

3. When the kite is in the air, the wings and the diamond part of the kite bend backward, forming a keel or breast to the wind.

4. See Chapter XXIII, The Minneapolis City-Wide Kite Tournament.

Questions

1. Is bamboo an easy material to work with?

2. Why is bamboo desirable in the construction of certain types of kite?

3. What is rice-paper made from?

THE MINNEAPOLIS CITY-WIDE KITE TOURNAMENT

AS IN THE case of the Annual Regatta for the boy builders of model boats, the Annual Kite Tournament is a gala event, which is looked forward to with keen anticipation by all kite enthusiasts. At some time during each summer, usually in July, the Recreation Department of the Minneapolis Park Board conducts a City-Wide Kite Tournament.

For the benefit of readers who may be interested in planning and managing such a Tournament, I submit the set of Rules and Regulations which have evolved out of our many years of study of this project, and which we find very satisfactory, as follows:

RULES AND REGULATIONS

I. Time and Place

The City-Wide Tournament is scheduled for Friday, July 12th, at 2:00 p. m., at the Parade Grounds, located between Kenwood and Superior Boulevard.

II. Who May Compete

All events are open to both boys and girls under 16 years of age, who reside in and near Minneapolis.

III. Events

1. Construction:
   (a) The most artistic kite.
   (b) Airplanes, gliders, and other in-inventions.
   (c) Messengers and parachutes.

2. Flying:
   (a) Kites 3 feet and over, strongest puller
   (b) Kites 3 feet and over, highest flyer in 10 minutes.
   (c) Kites under 3 feet, strongest puller.
   (d) Kites under 3 feet, highest flyer in 10 minutes.
   (e) Box-kites, strongest puller.
   (f) Box-kites, highest flyer in 10 minutes.

IV. Prizes

Preliminary Neighborhood Meets. Gold, silver, and bronze medals will be awarded to the first, second, and third place winners, respectively, on each playground.

City-Wide Tournament. A silver cup will be awarded to each first, second, and third place winner.

V. Suggestions

1. To stimulate interest in the kite-construction classes, and in the City-Wide Tournament, it is suggested that each playground hold a Preliminary Neighborhood Meet one week before the date of the City-Wide Tournament.

2. Hold a Neighborhood Kite Exhibition.

3. Hold the Preliminary Neighborhood Kite-Flying Meet on the same day as the Exhibition.

4. If possible, secure some big-hearted neighborhood booster with a truck to take

the boys and their kites to the Parade Grounds on the afternoon of the City-Wide Tournament.

5. If invited, the Dads of a number of the boys will be glad to assist in making the kites.

6. If enough adult kite-makers can be secured, start a construction class in the evening.

7. The City Library offers many splendid books, pamphlets, and magazines on how to build and fly kites.

8. Keep the bulletin-boards full of information, suggestions, and ideas on the construction of kites, and on the coming Neighborhood and City-Wide Meets.

9. Notify the Director of the Recreation Department if any unusual feature develops that can be used in newspaper publicity.

10. Be free to call upon the Recreation Department for assistance at any time.

VI. Final Instructions to Playground Instructors

1. All instructors are to report to Baseball Diamond No. 1, at the Parade Grounds, with their contestants and kites, promptly at 1:45 p. m., Friday, July 12th. Be prepared to hand in the following information: Number of boys; Number of girls; Number of kites. Report to the registration clerks, giving the complete list of kites. If a contestant is entering kites in more than one class, he should report the number of kites in each class.

2. After registration, all contestants with kites are to assemble on the bleachers of Diamond No. 1, to be judged in the "construction" events, and to receive assignments and instruction for the "flying" events.

3. At a given signal, all contestants with kites will assemble at the places designated, and kites will not take the air until the starting-signal is given.

4. At the end of 10 minutes, a signal will be given, at which time the kite highest in the air in each event will be declared winner.

5. Judges will start judging the hardest pullers immediately after this event.

6. Scoring and judging: First place, 5 points; Second place, 3 points; Third place, 1 point.

7. New inventions: Special new features, such as novelty kites or flying machines, will receive appropriate recognition.

8. Kite hospital: Boys should bring with them extra sticks, paper, string, and other parts, for use in case of accidents to kites. A suitable place on the field will be designated, where damaged kites may be repaired.

9. No kite will be permitted to take the air until all judging in the "construction" contests has been completed.